THE
Truly Healthy Pescatarian
COOKBOOK

THE
Truly Healthy
Pescatarian
COOKBOOK

75 FRESH & DELICIOUS RECIPES
TO MAINTAIN A HEALTHY WEIGHT

Nicole Hallissey
MS, RDN, CDN

ROCKRIDGE
PRESS

Interior Designer: Jamison Spittler
Cover Designer: William Mack
Photo Art Director: Sue Smith
Editor: Brian Hurley
Production Editor: Erum Khan

Photography: © 2018 Marija Vidal, Food styling by Cregg Green, cover, pp. x, 28; © 2018 Nadine Greeff, all interior photography except pp. x, 28.

ISBN: Print 978-1-64152-312-7 | eBook 978-1-64152-313-4

 I want to dedicate this book to my daughter, Leila. You've been

the greatest blessing in my life. Even though you're only a toddler, you have

contributed to this book enormously. Thank you for accompanying me

on many trips to the grocery store, helping cook the recipes while sitting

on our countertop, and most important, for being an honest and willing

taste tester. Cheers to the memories we've made in our kitchen and to the

lifetime of memories ahead of us. My life and heart have never been fuller.

I love you, my little Leila bean!

Contents

Introduction

Imagine waking up each morning with a strong and lean body, pliable joints, and a clear mind. How different would your life be? You would have energy to welcome the day and all it has to offer. It's important to realize that the food you eat can deliver these powerful benefits, allowing you to live up to your maximum potential. Life is too short to be sick, stressed, and inflamed.

Adopting a pescatarian diet is life changing. As a dietitian, I witness the benefits firsthand with my clients. This style of eating is slimming, is anti-inflammatory, and can protect your joints, brain, and heart from many ailments and degenerative diseases. This is what you will gain by reading and cooking from *The Truly Healthy Pescatarian Cookbook*.

I decided to write it because there has been a recent influx of clients who are asking for more fish recipes and more ways to eat plant-based meals. I don't think of myself as strictly a pescatarian, but I would describe myself as a plant- and fish-loving omnivore. I love fish. I cook and eat fish so often that the thought of writing a pescatarian cookbook was a no-brainer. To give you a taste of what to expect, the recipes in this book are plant-forward, fiber-rich, anti-inflammatory dishes that don't have too much sugar and contain a balance of foods from the land and sea.

Not a pescatarian? Don't worry, you don't have to be one to reap the benefits of this cookbook. I am excited to share these recipes because anyone can benefit from adapting this diet, whether you are already a pescatarian, an aspiring pescatarian, a vegetarian who wants to start including fish, or someone who eats everything. You don't even have to like fish, because I will show you some recipes that will change your mind. I love converting non–fish eaters into fish lovers! This book will help you navigate the sea to find a fish dish that you will love.

In this book, I will use the terms *diet* and *lifestyle* interchangeably. Many people think of a "diet" as something you go on and off of or something that is restrictive—it bullies the mind, always reminding you of the foods that are off-limits. When I use the term *diet* to describe the pescatarian diet, I want you to think of it not only as a way of eating but as a way of living. A *lifestyle* is something that is supported by behaviors, making the adopted changes easier to sustain for the long haul. It goes beyond your plate. It includes things like exercise, stress management, and self-care. I want to help you develop behaviors to make eating healthfully a no-brainer. No one deserves to be tormented by the "diet" mentality.

The content and recipes in this book will give you a new sense of well-being. In addition to the 75 mouth-watering and healthy recipes, you will learn about the pescatarian diet, how to turn your kitchen into a pescatarian haven, and how to find and maintain your healthy weight naturally. *The Truly Healthy Pescatarian Cookbook* is more than a compilation of recipes—it's a reservoir of knowledge to help change your mind-set about healthy eating and weight loss. What are you waiting for? Let's dive in!

1

The Truly Healthy Pescatarian Diet

What Is the Pescatarian Diet?

Very simply put, a pescatarian diet is a vegetarian diet with the added benefits of seafood. Pescatarians avoid eating red meat and poultry; instead they focus on a wide array of protein sources from the sea, including fish, shrimp, clams, and all other types of shellfish. There really isn't a set definition of this diet; what I love most is that everyone has their own interpretation of it. For instance, some pescatarians also include eggs and dairy, while others choose not to. In this book, we will be using eggs and dairy.

The pescatarian lifestyle allows you to individualize your food choices. One of the best and most important aspects of this diet is the balance of fruits, vegetables, whole grains, complex starches, healthy fats, nuts, seeds, legumes, and seafood. To help explain this diet, here is a list of its five major principles:

1. **Plant Forward:** This diet is mostly plant-based, meaning plant-based foods should take up most of your plate. In fact, at least half of your plate should be made up of vegetables at most meals. This comes out to about two handfuls of vegetables, or about 2 cups at each meal.

2. **Fiber Rich:** The fiber richness of this lifestyle will keep you full and satisfied. To reap the benefits of fiber, your focus should be on whole grains, complex carbohydrates, and of course, tons of fruits and vegetables.

3. **Healthy Fats:** Olive oil, avocados, nuts, and seeds are included in this diet because they contain healthy fats. These plant-based fats are mostly composed of monounsaturated fats, a type of fat that has been shown to have cardioprotective properties.

4. **Lean Proteins:** Most fish and other seafood are naturally lean, making it easy to choose heart-healthy proteins. And the fattier kinds of fish contain healthy fats that are found in a very small selection of foods. In fact, the fats in fish make this one of the most heart-healthy diets out there.

5. **Properly Portioned and Balanced:** The pescatarian lifestyle is a fun, creative, balanced, and satisfying way to eat. It will change the way you think about dieting.

I hope the above principles of the pescatarian diet have helped you better understand what it is. Let's delve a little further into some questions that I often get about the pescatarian diet and how to transition to a pescatarian diet from the standard American diet.

Do I need to cut out any food groups? No way! In fact, cutting out food groups is a major red flag when it comes to following certain diets. A beautiful thing about the pescatarian diet is that it includes all food groups: fruits, vegetables, proteins, grains, and dairy. Yes, carbs and fats are allowed!

What if someone in my family doesn't like fish? I say serve it anyway! The health benefits of eating fish make it worth cooking up even if one or two people in your family don't necessarily care for fish. It's possible that your non–fish lover may develop a taste for fish after repeated exposures. And if not, it means healthy leftovers for you!

What if I'm a newly converted pescatarian and my taste for fish is still developing? If you can relate to this question, don't worry—this is a good thing. I work with so many clients who repeatedly say they want to eat more fish. Many people grew up not regularly eating fish, and therefore it will just take time to develop the taste for it. Fish can also be intimidating to cook even though it's one of the easiest proteins to whip up. I always recommend starting with the milder-tasting fish and shellfish options, like shrimp and white-fleshed fish, and then slowly becoming more adventurous. When it comes to trying new foods, it takes a handful of experiences and preparations to really find your groove.

When I follow diets, I'm always hungry. Will I be hungry on this diet? This is probably the most common question I get as a dietitian. Warning: Most diets make you hungry! They restrict your calories, which will naturally increase your appetite at first. Not to mention, they can play mind games on you by making you think you need more food when you don't. But the way I designed this cookbook (with recipes containing lean protein, vegetables, and fiber) will prevent you from ever feeling underfed. Also, if you feel peckish, that's a sign you should probably eat. No one following this cookbook will go hungry—I promise!

How often do I have to eat seafood? The nice thing about the pescatarian lifestyle is that you can choose from a variety of protein sources, not just fish and shellfish. Being a pescatarian does not mean you must eat fish every day. Instead, you can eat what you are in the mood for and just know that fish is always an option. There are some general guidelines for the recommended frequency of fish consumption. These guidelines are created to make sure you eat fish in a safe and sustainable way that is good for your body and the environment. We will delve more into this later.

Will I still get enough protein if I cut out red meat and poultry? While red meat and poultry are significant sources of protein, you will easily be able to get more than enough protein following a pescatarian diet. Fish and shellfish contain very similar amounts of protein per gram as red meat and poultry. In addition, you will be able to get ample protein from dairy foods, like Greek yogurt, milk, and cottage cheese, as well as from vegetable sources, like tofu, tempeh, edamame, nuts, beans, and legumes.

Will it be difficult to find the fish and shellfish items at my grocery store? Not at all! I chose and developed the recipes in the book based on what local grocery stores have in stock—no exotic or hard-to-find fish or shellfish in this book.

Can I follow the pescatarian diet and still lose or maintain my weight? Of course. It's important to remember that losing weight can be done through many ways. Research shows that one of the most important components of a diet (besides calorie restriction) is adherence. Most diets work in the short term but are hard to maintain for a longer period because they are difficult for individuals to sustain. This diet is great because adherence is easy. It's easy to always eat the foods you love, and the pescatarian diet will give you a wide variety of foods to keep things fun.

Will cooking fish stink up my kitchen? Believe it or not, fresh fish does not smell fishy. If it does, it's likely too old. Fresh fish should have a mild smell. Some fish, like salmon and sardines, are more potent than others. If this is a concern to you, I would recommend turning on your stove fan, opening some windows, and cooking the fish with other delicious, potent ingredients, like garlic and onions—almost everyone likes these common cooking aromas. Or you can always grill the fish outside.

How do I know the pescatarian diet is the right diet for me? This is the perfect plan for you if you are currently avoiding or are trying to avoid red meat and poultry or want to include more fish and plants in your diet. You should develop more of a pescatarian diet if you want a diet that is energizing, satisfying, anti-inflammatory, and heart protective.

FINDING THE RIGHT PORTION

To make this eating plan enjoyable, it is important to not eat too much or too little. Feeling stuffed and feeling famished are two very uncomfortable feelings. One of the most important aspects of eating in general is to pay attention to your hunger and fullness cues. It sounds easy, but this can be very difficult to do for many reasons. Simply, I want you to eat when you are hungry and stop when you are satisfied—not stuffed. Eat enough but not too much. Eat often but not too often.

Serving Sizes for Common Foods

It can be helpful—and eye opening—to be aware of the portions you eat. Here are some serving-size guidelines to follow:

Equivalent	Food	Calories
Fist (¾ cup)	Rice	150
	Pasta	150
	Potatoes	150
Palm (4 ounces)	Lean meat	160
	Fish	160
	Poultry	160
Handful (1 ounce)	Nuts	170
	Raisins	85
Thumb (1 ounce)	Peanut butter	170
	Hard cheese	100

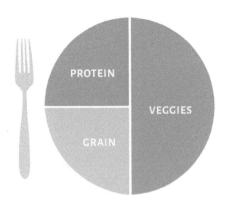

This brings me to the importance of portion size. Knowing the recommended portion size is super useful when trying to maintain weight or lose weight. I always suggest measuring out foods based on the serving recommendation. Serving sizes change based on what food you are eating. One of the best ways to become more aware of portion sizes is to read food labels. Properly measuring your food is an important factor when it comes to losing weight. Without understanding what a portion is, it's easy to eat too much. Our perceptions of serving sizes have been skewed by the massive portions that we are served when we eat out. The practice of measuring and being mindful of servings will help you recalibrate your perception to better understand what is considered a proper portion of food.

Measuring can be done with standard measuring cups and measuring spoons, like the ones you bake with. You can also use a scale for foods that are measured in ounces, like protein. If you choose to skip the tools, there are a few different methods that can help you become more familiar with portions. A rule of thumb (no pun intended) for estimating serving size is to use your hands.

You can also use your plate, or what I like to call the plate method. This bulletproof method allows you to eat all foods while keeping portions reasonable.

First, divide your plate in half. Fill half your plate with nonstarchy vegetables. Then fill 25 percent with whole grains or starchy vegetables and the remaining 25 percent with lean, filling protein.

When half your plate is made up of delicious nonstarchy vegetables and a quarter of your plate is full of lean, juicy protein, you have more wiggle room to eat the carbs that you love, like crusty bread or macaroni and cheese. Whether your plate contains fiber-rich whole grains or carb-filled classics, you can still feel satisfied, eat less, and lose weight when it's properly balanced with vegetables and lean protein. The pescatarian diet is not about restricting what you eat; it's about creating a sustainable way to eat.

The Science Behind the Pescatarian Diet

You may be wondering how you might benefit from the pescatarian diet. There are so many different diets and styles of eating out there—what makes one better than the rest? To answer those questions, let's look at the facts. This diet, unlike so many diets out there, is backed by science. Here is what science is telling us:

Eating fish helps fight inflammation. *Inflammation* is a huge buzzword in the media when it comes to health. To a certain degree, an inflammatory response, triggered by our immune systems, is essential to fighting off foreign invaders, such as microbes or chemicals. But for some people who eat the standard American diet, inflammation can persist in low levels over time. This is referred to as chronic inflammation. Diet- and lifestyle-related diseases, like obesity, heart disease, diabetes, arthritis, and cancer, all have one thing in common: chronic inflammation.

How can the pescatarian diet fight inflammation? Unlike the standard American diet, the pescatarian diet includes foods that do just that. Omega-3 fats—which have anti-inflammatory benefits—are essential to our health and abundant in only a few foods, fish being one of them. One of the easiest and best ways to ensure you are consuming sufficient omega-3s is to eat a variety of fish, especially fatty fish. The pescatarian diet also encompasses plant foods, like fruits, veggies, whole grains, and legumes, which all have antioxidants and polyphenols—powerful, health-boosting plant compounds. The basic principles of the pescatarian diet, along with exercise, sleep, and stress reduction, synergistically work together to crush chronic inflammation.

Omega-3s Come From the Sea

These super healthy fats can vary according to type of fish and whether the fish was farm raised or wild caught. Wild-caught fish acquire and accumulate omega-3s in their tissue when they eat phytoplankton that consume microalgae. Farmed fish acquire them if they are given feed that is fortified with omega-3s. Fattier fish, like salmon, mackerel, sardines, tuna, and herring, contain higher amounts of omega-3s than leaner fish, like tilapia, bass, and cod.

Eating fish protects your heart. Eating fish lowers your risk of heart disease, lowers your triglycerides, and lowers your blood pressure. One of the first studies to explore the heart-health benefits of omega-3s found that men who were advised to eat fish twice a week after surviving a heart attack had a 29 percent reduction in all-cause mortality compared with men who were not advised to eat fish. It's not surprising that populations that eat a lot of fish, like in Japan and certain Mediterranean regions, have fewer heart attacks. Simply put, the research shows that if you eat fish, you live longer.

Eating fish boosts your brainpower. Did you know that the brain is nearly 60 percent fat? Fatty acids play an important role in brain development and performance. In fact, an omega-3 fatty acid found in fish, docosahexaenoic acid (DHA), plays an integral role in neurotransmitter communication, membrane fluidity, and brain cell repair. Researchers are still connecting the dots to learn more about the positive effects of omega-3s on mood and behavioral disorders, depression, and Alzheimer's disease. What is known is that omega-3s are essential for brain health. That's enough to make eating fish a no-brainer for me.

Eating fish helps you trim your waistline. This makes sense when you consider the two things that fish does not have: tons of calories and saturated fats. Compared with red meats, fish (even the varieties highest in fat) have fewer calories and less saturated fat. Research has shown that body mass index (BMI) increases as the amount of animal protein in the diet increases. This is why it is never particularly shocking to me when studies find that people who follow vegetarian and pescatarian diets have lower BMIs than individuals who do not. When you follow a pescatarian diet, you will naturally eat foods that are appetite-quelling, which makes it much easier to maintain a healthy weight, lose weight, or prevent weight gain.

Eating fish does not give you mercury poisoning. I get asked about fish and mercury a lot—especially by pregnant women. My answer is you can eat fish without getting mercury poisoning. For children and pregnant women, just eat lower-mercury-containing varieties, such as canned light tuna, salmon, pollock, and catfish. Fish high in mercury tend to be larger, predatory fish, like shark, swordfish, tilefish, mackerel, and bigeye tuna. For everyone else, just eat a variety, in the right portions and at the recommended frequency. Most health professionals would agree that the benefits of eating fish outweigh the potential risks. This is especially true for children and developing fetuses, given that omega-3s are essential during times of brain development.

Fish and Shellfish Highest in Omega-3 Fatty Acids (per 3 ounces)	
Herring, Atlantic, cooked, dry heat	1,712 mg
Salmon, Atlantic, wild, cooked, dry heat	1,564 mg
Whitefish, mixed species, cooked, dry heat	1,370 mg
Anchovies, European, raw	1,231 mg
Mackerel, Atlantic, cooked, dry heat	1,091 mg
Halibut, Greenland, cooked, dry heat	1,001 mg
Rainbow trout, wild, cooked, dry heat	840 mg
Sardines, Atlantic, canned in oil, drained solids with bones	825 mg
Striped bass, cooked, dry heat	822 mg
Tuna, white, canned in water, drained solids	733 mg
Mussels, blue, cooked, moist heat	665 mg
Sea bass, mixed species, cooked, dry heat	648 mg

Source: U.S. Department of Agriculture Food Composition Databases

The Pescatarian Diet and Your Health

Let's compare the pescatarian diet with the standard American diet, which is characterized by the intake of fatty and highly processed meats, refined grains, sugary beverages, and other processed foods. Not to mention, there is a big problem with portion distortion. Not only are these foods commonly consumed; they're taking over our plates in larger-than-life portions. The Western diet lacks fruits, vegetables, lean protein, whole grains, and yes, fish. Our total average fish consumption is only half the recommended amount, and only 1 in 10 Americans eat enough fruits and vegetables. These poor eating habits contribute to a long list of pro-inflammatory diseases. In contrast to the standard American diet, the pescatarian diet, when done right, is swimming in health benefits. Let's dive into the reasons why:

It's more flexible than a vegetarian or vegan diet: The vegan diet calls for the exclusion of all animal products—even honey. There are multiple versions of the vegetarian diet; some versions include dairy and eggs, and others don't. What all variations of the vegetarian diet have in common is the exclusion of animal flesh. Some people refer to the pescatarian diet as a pesco-vegetarian diet, which is a vegetarian diet that includes fish and shellfish. When following a pescatarian diet, you will have greater flexibility than when following a vegan or vegetarian diet. You'll have the freedom to choose from oodles of healthy protein sources, like fish, seafood, eggs, and dairy. This makes it easier to get dense but lean protein, vitamins, minerals, and healthy fats.

It's plant forward: This diet focuses on what we could all use a little more of: plants. The plant-forwardness of this diet encourages you to consume a variety of filling and nutrient-rich fruits, veggies, whole grains, nuts, seeds, beans, and other legumes.

Fish Consumption Recommendations

One of the most common recommendations for fish consumption comes from the American Heart Association, which recommends eating fish, particularly fatty fish, at least twice a week. This recommendation considers 1 serving of fish as 3½ ounces cooked or about ¾ cup flaked.

Pro-Inflammatory Foods Found in the Standard American Diet	Anti-Inflammatory Foods Found in the Pescatarian Diet
Refined carbohydrates: Soda, white bread, and pastries	Fatty fish: Salmon, tuna, mackerel, and sardines
Fried foods: French fries, fried meats	Olive oil
Red meat: Burgers, steaks	Nuts: Almonds, pistachios, and walnuts
Processed meats: Hot dogs, sausages, and deli meats	Fruits: Blueberries, strawberries, cherries, and citrus fruits
Less healthy fats: Margarine, shortening, and lard	Green leafy veggies: Spinach, kale, bok choy, and collards

It's full of fiber: Our bodies work better when we eat enough fiber. A sufficient fiber intake of 25 to 38 grams has been shown to improve digestion, stabilize blood sugar levels, lower cholesterol and blood pressure, reduce food cravings, and boost satiety.

It's lower in saturated fat: Fish has only tiny amounts of saturated fats, also known as the bad fats. Animal protein, on the other hand—particularly in red meat and the dark meat of poultry—contributes to higher amounts of saturated fats. Replacing saturated fats with the healthy fats found in fish has been linked to decreased risk of heart disease.

It's great for weight loss: When done the right way and in the right portions, foods that make up this diet can help you lose weight—and keep it off! We will take a much closer look into how this diet is great for weight loss in chapter 3, "Finding and Maintaining Your Naturally Healthy Weight" (page 29).

It's packed with nutrients: In addition to containing protein and anti-inflammatory fats, fish and shellfish are packed with vitamins and minerals, including iron, calcium, vitamin D, potassium, selenium, magnesium, zinc, and iodine.

It helps lower your carbon footprint: The consumption of meat—especially red meat—is a major contributor to harmful greenhouse gases. Avoiding meat, eating more plant-based foods, and including the right amount of fish are a win-win for both your health and the environment.

You'll feel happier: Living the pescatarian lifestyle will put a pep in your step. The proper amount of nutrients along with the balance of exercise, sleep, and stress management will do wonders for your mood, energy level, and overall happiness.

It's a brilliant choice for your brain: Imagine, no more brain fog! The healthy fats from eating fish are integral to brain health. Even during pregnancy, it's known that omega-3s offer enormous benefits to your baby's brain development.

2

Your Pescatarian Kitchen

Ingredients

Setting yourself up to follow a healthy pescatarian diet means having a plan and sticking to it. Success starts with a well-equipped kitchen. You will need the proper arsenal of kitchen staples and the right equipment. Having a well-stocked kitchen is a necessity and a total lifesaver when cooking an abundance of vegetables, fish, and plant proteins. Aromatic herbs and spices will excite your taste buds while allowing you to keep things appetizing and interesting. Having a few different cooking oils handy will add some variety in flavor. Using various whole grains will keep things fun by providing different textures. Using your freezer will allow you to put dinner on the table quickly and easily, and it will help you reduce food waste. If this sounds like a lot to master, don't worry. This chapter is going to be all about setting up your pescatarian kitchen so you can cook healthy food in an easy way. To start, here are the ingredients that I've found most useful to have in my pantry, refrigerator, and freezer while on the pescatarian diet.

THE PESCATARIAN PANTRY

Spices: My go-to spices for fish include kosher salt and sea salt, curry powder, Old Bay Seasoning, Italian seasoning, dried oregano, ground turmeric, chili powder, paprika, and ground cumin. Grocery stores offer fantastic spice blends that are great for curries or chili. Most blends are perfectly fine to use and can save you time, but just make sure they don't have too much salt. I always opt for salt-free blends and then add my own salt while cooking. Your spice preferences may be different, and that's okay! Whichever spices you choose to stock your pantry with will translate into beautifully flavored dishes that fit your personal preference.

Whole Grains: Although I cook with a variety of whole grains, my favorites are quinoa, freekeh, bulgur, wheat berries, and brown rice. Each of these whole grains is loaded with fiber and B vitamins, two things that refined white grains are lacking. To save time, I cook grains in bulk and store them in the refrigerator to throw in salads, soups, and stews or simply just have as a side with a piece of fish.

Beans: Beans are among the most nutritious and affordable plant proteins. I always keep lentils in the pantry, which cook super quickly and are great to add to soups and salads. Other beans, like chickpeas, black beans, kidney beans, and white beans, are easy additions to chili, casseroles, salads, and pasta dishes. You can buy dried or canned beans; use whichever you prefer. When buying canned beans, look for no salt added or low sodium. Grocery stores are now offering beans in shelf-stable and frozen bags, which are also a major time-saver. A newer obsession of mine is pasta made out of beans. Local supermarkets are now offering a variety of bean pastas that are made with chickpeas, lentils, edamame, or black beans. Most bean pastas are loaded with way more protein and fiber and tend to be naturally gluten-free, but be sure to always check the label.

Canned Items: Three of my favorite canned items for cooking fish are canned coconut milk (either reduced fat or full fat) for curries, reduced-sodium vegetable stock for soups, and fire-roasted tomatoes for quick and flavorful sauces.

Nuts: I always keep pistachios, pine nuts, almonds, and walnuts handy. I do switch things up by buying them whole, slivered, or chopped. Besides noshing on these during the day, I love adding them to salads for an extra crunch, throwing them in the blender with greens for a creamy pesto, or toasting them on the stove top for their nutty and decadent flavor.

Other Shelf-Stable Staples: I buy a variety of salsas, like tomato salsa, salsa verde, and mango salsa, to throw on top of a salad, in a chili, or on top of a piece of fish. I also have a few nut butters, like peanut butter and cashew butter, to make creamy sauces and dressings.

Oils: My four favorite cooking oils are olive oil, avocado oil, coconut oil, and sesame oil (in no particular order). Switching up your oil can make a world of a difference in aroma and flavor when cooking fish and vegetables. I also like using butter—real butter! A little bit of butter makes fish taste amazing. When you rotate among a variety of healthy plant oils, using butter here and there is okay on the pescatarian diet. See, I told you that the pescatarian way of eating was awesome!

Vinegars: The three vinegars I always have on hand are apple cider vinegar, balsamic vinegar, and red wine vinegar. I love using them in dressings and sauces. I also like champagne vinegar.

THE PESCATARIAN REFRIGERATOR

Tofu: Tofu is a great addition to almost any meal and can even be eaten raw when added to spring rolls, salads, or smoothies—yes, even smoothies! It's great at absorbing flavors. What I love most about tofu is its versatility.

Tempeh: Tempeh is a meat substitute made with fermented soybeans and grains. It has more protein and fiber than tofu, and it's great for stir-fries or crumbled up in chilis.

Eggs: Eggs are easy, versatile, and inexpensive. They are a great source of pescatarian-friendly protein to keep handy.

Chia Seeds, Hemp Seeds, and Ground Flaxseed: All three of these seeds offer healthy fats, protein, fiber, and crunch. They're great to add to smoothies, salads, yogurts, and oatmeal. Chia seeds do not have much flavor, while hemp seeds and ground flaxseed taste nutty. It's recommended to keep hemp seeds and ground flaxseed in the refrigerator to preserve their delicate fats. Chia seeds can be stored in your pantry, but I keep them in the refrigerator with my other seeds.

Fresh Herbs: I have at least one or two bunches of fresh herbs in my refrigerator at all times. My favorite herbs are parsley, cilantro, oregano, and rosemary. I store them wrapped with damp paper towels in sealed plastic bags.

Citrus: Fish tastes so much better with fresh citrus! Fresh lemon, lime, or orange juice tastes great when squeezed on top of fish or used to make a zesty sauce or dressing.

Fruits and Vegetables: When choosing fruits and veggies, variety is key! Eating a rainbow of different fruits and vegetables will not only add a beautiful touch to your plate but also ensure that you are getting essential nutrients, antioxidants, and phytonutrients— powerful plant compounds that are important for your health.

Fresh Fish: Unless I have a very specific craving for a certain type of fish, I buy whatever is on sale in my local grocery store. When looking for fish, I consider price, freshness, and sustainability, which I'll touch upon later (page 20).

THE PESCATARIAN FREEZER

Frozen Fruits and Vegetables: The consensus among dietitians is that frozen fruits and veggies are no better or worse than fresh. Using frozen produce eliminates some common barriers to eating fresh produce, making it easier for people to eat more fruits and veggies. With frozen produce, you don't have to wash, peel, or cut—all of those steps are done for you! When buying frozen produce, just be conscious of and try to avoid any extra sauces, cheeses, or salt, as well as added sugar with frozen fruit.

Frozen Grains: For the past few years I've heavily relied on precooked frozen grains, like brown rice and quinoa. No cooking or extra pans required, which means fewer dirty dishes. Most frozen grains can be microwaved in the bag—just check the label.

Frozen Fish: Sometimes I buy extra fresh fish if it's on sale and immediately freeze it. Other times I buy frozen fish fillets or frozen shrimp. Some supermarkets even have fully cooked frozen fish and shellfish, which is a total time-saver. I love using precooked frozen shrimp for salads and stir-fries.

Leftovers: My freezer is indispensable for leftovers. Over the years I have learned that almost everything is freezable. I love freezing leftover soups, stews, risottos, and veggie burgers. Freezing foods can also help reduce food waste. Throughout this book, I'll point out which recipes freeze well.

Equipment

Having the right equipment will make your time in the kitchen a lot more enjoyable. You won't need anything fancy, just staples that you probably already have. If you don't have something on this list, there is probably an alternative way to reach your end goal. Here are my top five recommendations for kitchen equipment:

1. **Sturdy Nonstick Baking Sheets:** Many of the recipes in this book are baked or roasted. Having at least two baking sheets will allow you to create sheet-pan meals that are quick and require very little cleanup.

2. **Stainless Steel, Nonstick, or Cast-Iron Skillet:** While it is great to have all of these items, you can definitely get away with just one. They are often inexpensive. I recommend buying a pan that is large enough to make one-pot meals, which there are a lot of in this cookbook.

3. **Sharp Knives:** Good-quality knives are a necessity for cutting fruits, vegetables, and protein with ease. I personally like ceramic knives for fruits and vegetables, but stainless-steel knives with a sturdy handle will do the trick.

4. **Blender, Immersion Blender, or Food Processor:** Blenders and immersion blenders are suitable for making soups, dressings, and smoothies. A food processor can make soups and dressings but is not ideal for smoothies. You can choose which one works best for your personal preference.

5. **Durable Food-Storage Containers:** My life changed when I got rid of my flimsy plastic containers. I recommend either glass or BPA-free plastic containers in all shapes and sizes. Having good containers will make prepping, storing, freezing, and packing food a lot easier.

Here are two other pieces of equipment that I recommend but are not necessary:

Vegetable Spiralizer: This gadget makes noodles out of vegetables, like zucchini or carrots. If you do not have one, you can easily use a veggie peeler to make veggie ribbons.

Slow Cooker: This is a kitchen staple for me. It makes one-pot meals that require very little cleanup. However, anything that is made in a slow cooker can also be made on the stove.

Cooking Seafood Like a Pro

Cooking seafood is easier than you think. Let's go over some best practices for choosing, preparing, cooking, and storing fish and shellfish.

PICKING SEAFOOD

Choosing seafood from your local market or grocery store is easy when you have a sense of what to look for. Finding the best-quality fish and shellfish requires using all your senses. Here are 10 tips to help you:

1. Inspect the fillet to ensure there are no separations or cracks in the flesh.

2. When gently poked, the flesh should be firm and the indentation from your finger should spring back to its original shape. Flesh that is mushy or soft and remains dented from your finger is a sign that the fish is old.

3. For whole fish, the skin should be firm, shiny, metallic, and moist. Check the gills to ensure they are pinkish red. The eyes should be moist, clear, and slightly bulging. Avoid eyes that are discolored, cloudy, or sunken.

4. Smell the fish. If it smells fishy, it's not fresh. Fresh fish should never have a strong fishy smell. Since it's from the ocean, a salty, briny smell can be expected.

5. Check the color of the fillet, which can vary based on the type of fish. Fish fillets should have no patches, discoloration, or drying around the edges. If visible, the veins of the fish should appear red, not gray or dark brown. Only red-fleshed fish, such as tuna, will have dark veins.

6. When buying mussels and clams, look to make sure shells are not cracked or dis-colored. Most of the shells should be closed. If any of them are open, a slight tap on the shell should close it, ensuring that the creature is alive. Discard shells that don't close when tapped. Always wash thoroughly. For mussels, scrub the outside of the shells and remove the beard. For clams, soak for 10 minutes in cold water, which will remove the salt inside. After being cooked, the clams and mussels should open. Discard ones that do not open.

7. Find out the seafood's origins. It's always good practice to know where your food comes from. Fish from the supermarket should always be labeled to let you know where it was caught. If possible, it's always best to choose ingredients that are locally sourced. My go-to sustainability guide for fish and shellfish is the Monterey Bay Aquarium Seafood Watch. You can download a PDF version of the guide or even use the app on your phone while shopping. See Resources (page 153).

8. At the supermarket or fishmonger, fish should be stored in crushed ice in a perforated pan. Grocery-store fish shelves are usually perforated so the water from melting ice can drain. After purchasing the fish, be sure to cook it within two days.

9. Opt for wild over farmed. There are notable differences in farmed versus wild fish. When choosing farm-raised fish, make sure it's raised sustainably. In most cases, it is more sustainable and healthier to choose wild-caught fish.

10. Determine if the fish is fresh, frozen, or thawed. When a fish is labeled "fresh," it usually means it was never frozen. Don't get me wrong, though—just because fish is frozen doesn't mean it's not good to eat. You may also see fish labeled as "pre-viously frozen," which is fish that has been thawed to sell. No matter if it's frozen, previously frozen, or fresh, use the tips above to determine quality and freshness. Keep in mind, though, anything that has been previously frozen will have more moisture.

PREP, COOKING, AND STORAGE

Here are my top 10 tips for preparing, cooking, and storing seafood:

1. Refrigerate seafood on the bottom shelf right after bringing it home. Cook right away or up to 2 days after buying it. Always pat fish fillets dry with a paper towel before cooking.

2. When marinating a fillet, make sure not to let it sit too long if it contains acidic flavors from citrus or vinegar sources, as this can cook the seafood. Using a milder marinade for a shorter amount of time is recommended. A good rule of thumb is to marinate fish for 30 minutes to 2 hours in the refrigerator.

3. Make sure to season both sides of the fish, not just the top. It will taste better this way and ensure that every bite is super flavorful.

4. When sautéing fish, make sure the oil in the pan is hot enough before adding the fish. This will create a sear and prevent the fish from sticking to the pan.

5. For most fish cooked in a pan, cook it 70 percent on one side before gently flipping and lowering the heat. At this point, add herbs and aromatics to the pan and baste the fish with its drippings. The first side will be your presentation side.

6. Don't overcook! Fish should always be juicy and tender, not dry and tough. It should easily flake apart with a fork.

7. After the fish is removed from the pan or oven, allow it to rest for 2 to 3 minutes before serving. This allows the fish to retain moisture and finish cooking while resting.

8. Add some wine! Don't discard the flavor left in the pan when pan roasting or sautéing. You can easily use what's left in the pan to make a pan sauce by adding a splash of white wine, lemon juice, and olive oil. If you are feeling extra fancy, you can also add fresh herbs, a mashed garlic clove, and some shallots. The pan sauce can be made in the 2 to 3 minutes while your fish is resting.

9. Never leave cooked seafood out of the refrigerator for more than 2 hours.

10. Store leftover cooked fish in a dry, tightly sealed container in the coolest part of your refrigerator. The Food and Drug Administration recommends eating leftover fish within 3 to 4 days after being cooked.

COOKING THE WHOLE FISH

Buy whole fish scaled and gutted from the grocery store or your local fishmonger. I prefer to grill or bake whole fish. Make sure your grill or preheated oven is hot. Stuff the fish with herbs, aromatics, or sliced citrus. Oil and season the entire inside and outside of the fish. If grilling, you should flip the fish only once and cook it equally on both sides. Cooking times will vary based on the size and type of the fish. Don't touch fish after the initial sear. Moving the fish around too much will make the skin tear. Once done, let it rest for 2 to 3 minutes, then drizzle with olive oil and a squeeze of fresh citrus juice.

COOKING METHODS FOR FILLETS

There are many different cooking methods to choose from when it comes to eating the pescatarian way. Choosing the best method will depend mostly on the type of fish you have and what you're in the mood for. I can't even say that one method is easier or quicker than another, because they're all so easy and quick.

Pan Sautéing: Use a cast-iron skillet or a stainless-steel or nonstick sauté pan to cook fish in a little bit of oil on the stove over high heat. You can use the pan drippings to make a delicious and easy pan sauce after your fish is done cooking.

Oven Roasting or Baking: This method requires cooking the fish in the oven at a temperature of 350°F to 400°F. This method cooks the fish with dry air, which can jeopardize the moisture of the fish. Using a sauce and not overcooking it will reduce the loss of moisture.

Poaching: Poaching is when you submerge the fish in simmering liquid to cook. You can use water, but I love using veggie stock infused with fresh herbs, citrus, and aromatics because it adds flavor.

Searing: This technique cooks fish in a stainless-steel pan or cast-iron skillet at a high temperature. The piece of fish is cooked with the seasoned side or skin side down. It produces a crispy, delicious crust.

Steaming: This method cooks fish with water vapor in a closed vessel, usually with the fish laid on top of the upper part of a double saucepan with a perforated base. Placing the fish on a bed of fresh herbs will add an extra touch of flavor.

Grilling: As opposed to thin fillets, which dry up quickly when grilled, this method is best for thick fillets or steaks that can withstand the intense heat and retain their moisture. Swordfish, tuna, salmon, and mackerel are great fish to grill.

ADDING FLAVOR

Fish doesn't have to taste bland! With just the right touch of seasoning, it can be incredibly flavorful with not a lot of effort. To prove it, I've come up with 10 tips to add flavor to your fish. The first five tips are for matching flavor profiles of specific seafood items with complementary vegetables.

1. Fish fillets and scallops pair perfectly with a simple vegetable mash. Create a veggie mash by puréeing your favorite combination of cooked leeks, cauliflower, turnips, and/or sweet potatoes. Add your fish right on top of the mash for a perfect and healthy pairing.

2. Bake veggies, like broccoli, cauliflower, asparagus, carrots, or zucchini, in the oven right alongside your favorite fish fillets. Most fish fillets and veggies can bake at the same temperature for the same amount of time, which makes for the easiest dinner ever!

3. Salmon and shrimp are delicious when served with broccoli, red peppers, and sugar snap peas in a Chinese stir-fry. The best and most basic ingredients for a stir-fry include sesame oil, low-sodium soy sauce, ginger, and scallions.

4. Seafood and vegetables pair great together in curries. Curries are common in both Thai and Indian cuisines. There is nothing more flavorful than mussels or shrimp served in a coconut-lemongrass curry sauce with red peppers and broccoli. You can also use curry powder as a seasoning for all type of fish and shellfish, as well as veggies.

5. Add fish fillets, shrimp, clams, mussels, or scallops over spiralized veggie noodles instead of rice or pasta for a low-carb and tasty seafood dish. Vegetables noodles can be made with all types of veggies, like zucchini, carrots, broccoli stems, or beets.

And here are five tips for focusing on interesting and delicious ways to add a lot of flavor to any fish dish:

1. Use premixed spice blends. This is probably the quickest and easiest way to get deceptively complex flavor with the least amount of effort. My absolute favorite spice blend for fish fillets is Old Bay Seasoning. Check your grocery store for spice mixes.

2. Never underestimate the power of fresh herbs! I love pairing whitefish, scallops, and shellfish with fresh herbs like parsley, cilantro, thyme, and rosemary. Herbs are great for making pesto to pair with all types of fish.

3. Add some crunch to your fillet by mixing your favorite seasonings with bread crumbs. I love coating whitefish fillets with Old Bay–seasoned panko bread crumbs or coating salmon with bread crumbs mixed with finely chopped pistachios.

4. Keep fish marinades simple with salt, pepper, olive oil, and fresh lemon juice, or mix Dijon mustard with a dash of honey. Oh my, I'm already drooling!

5. You don't need exotic ingredients to cook flavorful fish. Ginger, shallots, and garlic are fantastic ways to introduce sophisticated aromatics to your cooking.

Seasonal and Affordable

There is a misconception that seafood is expensive. While some fish and shellfish options are more expensive than others, it doesn't have to be that way. Here are five ways to eat seafood without breaking the bank.

1. **Shop sales.** Buying fish that is on sale at your local grocery store or fish market will definitely help you save a few dollars. It will also prevent you from eating the same fish each week. Eating a variety of fish is better for you and the environment. Also, if you find a great sale on fish, you can buy a surplus, wrap it up tightly in aluminum foil or moisture-proof paper, and store it in the freezer for later use.

2. **Buy frozen.** Frozen fish tends to be less expensive than fresh. Grocery stores now sell frozen filleted fish in individual packets. Having fish handy in the freezer can save you time and money.

3. **Use a variety of canned fish.** Like canned tuna, you can find a number of other canned fish and shellfish items in your local grocery store. Canned salmon is great for salmon burgers, sardines and canned crab are great to put on salads, and canned clams can make a delicious sauce for pasta or zucchini noodles.

4. **Eat a variety of both fish and plant proteins.** Don't forget that following a pescatarian diet doesn't mean you must eat fish every day. Eating fish at least twice a week and using other affordable, sustainable plant proteins, like tofu, tempeh, and beans, will help keep your budget in check.

5. **Buy in-season fish.** You'll save money and get a better-quality product when you buy fish that is in season. It's also more sustainable for the environment. Seasonality of fish varies from year to year and is different depending on where you live. It's best to avoid buying fish during breeding or spawning times. The Marine Conservation Society offers a useful seasonal fish-buying guide that you can find online (see Resources on page 153).

3

Finding and Maintaining Your Naturally Healthy Weight

Your Healthy Weight

I'm sure you've heard of apps that calculate the calories you take in and burn in your daily life. Weight loss is achieved when you create a calorie deficit against your calorie needs. Simply put, you will lose weight if you burn more calories than you consume. You can put yourself in a calorie deficit in two ways: eating less, which is referred to as calorie restriction, and burning calories through physical activity and exercise. This equation makes weight loss sound so simple: Just eat fewer calories! Anyone who ever tried to lose weight knows it's not that easy, and that's because our lifestyles make it very difficult to eat less and exercise more.

So, you may be wondering: How do I know if I'm at a healthy weight? What should my ideal weight be? One very general, but not perfect, reference to help you determine your weight status is BMI. It's one of the more reliable indicators of weight status and health for the general population. Having a BMI that is too low or too high has been associated with a number of negative health outcomes.

All About BMI and BMR

Body mass index (BMI) is a measurement system to determine your weight-to-height proportion. It can help you see where you stand as you begin to formulate your weight-loss goals. To calculate your BMI, go to Webmd.com/diet/body-bmi-calculator.

The body needs a set number of calories just to stay alive and function normally. Your basal metabolic rate (BMR) is the amount of calories your body requires to perform life-sustaining functions, such as breathing, digesting food, and keeping your heart beating. These functions account for the largest amount of calories burned each day. Basically, BMR measures your metabolism or the amount of calories your body burns at rest. To calculate your BMR, visit Calculator.net/bmr-calculator.

BMI is an equation that uses your height-to-weight ratio. It is not accurate for everyone because it only measures body mass and does not tell you much past that. It does not break down bone mass, muscle mass, or fat mass. This means someone who has a lot of muscle and very little fat can have a high BMI when in reality this person is a perfectly healthy weight for his or her body type.

Like everything, there are dos and don'ts of using your BMI as a health indicator. Do use this tool as a general guideline to determine your weight status. Don't use it as a tell-all indicator of your overall health. There are plenty of people with normal BMIs who are unhealthy and plenty of people with higher BMIs who are perfectly healthy. If you are underweight, overweight, or obese, talk to your doctor for guidance on achieving a healthy weight. I would also recommend working with a registered dietitian nutritionist to help set goals and develop a plan that is right for you. The best approach to weight loss and weight maintenance is personal and specific to you.

Identifying Your Daily Caloric Intake

The first step to knowing how much you should be eating for weight loss or weight maintenance is determining how many calories your body needs each day. There are a few different ways to determine this; some calculations are more complicated than others. The easiest way to determine your calorie intake for the purposes of getting a rough estimate is to multiply your current weight by the number 12. Let's use an example of Suzie, who weighs 150 pounds and is 5 feet 2 inches tall. To determine Suzie's calories, multiply her weight by 12: $150 \times 12 = 1,800$.

In order for Suzie to maintain her weight, she would need to eat roughly 1,800 calories per day. Based on the BMI chart, Suzie is in the overweight category. It's important to remember that just because your BMI is in a specific category doesn't always mean you need to lose weight. Suzie can be perfectly healthy and fit at 150 pounds. If she would feel more comfortable at a lower weight or could benefit from weight loss for a specific health condition, she would have to put herself in a calorie deficit to lose weight. Depending on what is feasible for Suzie's lifestyle, a calorie deficit of 250 to 750 calories per day would suffice for weight loss. So let's say she wants to achieve a goal of 1,300 daily net calories, or a 500-calorie deficit. One way would be to eat 500 fewer calories per day. Another approach would be to achieve the deficit through a mixture of caloric restriction and exercise. Eating 250 fewer calories and exercising (for example, jogging for 30 minutes or even taking a brisk hour-long walk daily) to burn an additional 250 calories would result in the 500-calorie deficit. This means she could eat 1,550 calories a day. No matter what, I never recommend for anyone to eat fewer than 1,200 calories a day.

The pescatarian diet aligns perfectly with the most recent Dietary Guidelines for Americans, which are science-based recommendations to help Americans make informed choices about eating. Both the guidelines and the pescatarian diet emphasize a healthy eating pattern that includes fruits, vegetables, whole grains, and lean protein. The guidelines also recommend that we eat less sodium, saturated fats, and sugar. Fish is naturally low in all these things. Following a healthier eating pattern is the most powerful tool we have to reduce the onset of disease.

All Calories Are Not Created Equal

A calorie is a calorie, right? I have this discussion with a lot with clients. It's true, you can follow any diet you want and still lose weight, but only if you put yourself in a calorie deficit. But what is also true is that you may feel super crappy if you eat a calorie-restricted diet that doesn't provide you with all the essential nutrients. A 1,500-calorie diet adhering to the standard American diet is not the same as a 1,500-calorie pescatarian diet. Yes, both diets have the same number of calories, but there will be a drastic difference in the way that you feel when you eat them. When putting yourself in a calorie deficit for weight loss, it is more important than ever to get the most nutrients from the number of calories you consume. Dietitians refer to this as nutrient density. The pescatarian diet is among the most nutrient-dense diets and will easily give you the vitamins, minerals, healthy fats, fiber, lean protein, and all other nutrients that are essential to thrive and feel your best.

Factors That Influence Weight Loss

I've placed a lot of focus on calories, but I also want to stress the importance of other factors that can influence weight loss. These factors are just as important as calorie intake, so let's go over them below.

Hydration: Water helps boost satiety (the feeling of fullness), which can prevent over-eating. It's common for people to think they're hungry when in fact they just need water. When you feel hungry, grab a glass or bottle of water instead of diving into the refrigerator. This will fill your stomach and help you save some calories, even if you still need to eat after hydrating. Water also saves calories when it is consumed in place of higher-calorie beverages that have added sugar.

Sleep: Believe it or not, how much you snooze each night can affect your weight. Research shows that people who sleep less than seven hours per night tend to have higher BMIs. Lack of sleep has been shown to affect hormones that control appetite, making you feel hungrier. Staying up later each night also allows more hours to nosh. Last, lack of sleep leads to fatigue the next day, which results in decreased energy expenditure. For example, who really wants to take the stairs over the elevator when they're tired?

Exercise: Moving your body has remarkable benefits that go beyond creating a calorie deficit for weight management. Exercise has been linked to reduction in stress, depression, and anxiety thanks to the power of endorphins, the body's natural mood boosters. It is also crucial for heart health and disease management.

Stress: This factor has a big influence on your weight. Long-term stress has been linked to weight gain and increased appetite. This is likely due to a fluctuation in certain hormones, including one in particular called cortisol. This hormone not only makes your body store fat, but it increases fat in your midsection, also known as belly fat.

A Holistic Approach

Eating the pescatarian way is great for weight loss because it's an easy, satisfying, and balanced way of eating. Achieving a healthy weight is all about finding balance— balance not only in your calorie intake but also in hours of sleep, levels of stress, and exercise. When working with clients, I take a holistic approach to weight management. Sometimes we don't even talk about food in the first visit. When I understand the full picture, it helps me to better pinpoint the factors that are making it difficult for the client to lose weight.

Usually, the factors are unrelated or indirectly related to food. For example, stress and exhaustion typically result in emotional eating or eating to stay awake, whether people are conscious of it or not. Another common factor that interferes with weight loss is a busy schedule. I'm sure so many of you can relate to this one. When someone is spread too thin, it's difficult to find the time to plan your meals. Typically, when people are too busy, the first things that get chopped (no pun intended) are meal prep and home cooking. To compensate for the lack of home-cooked meals, people turn toward fast food and packaged, convenient meals to fill their bellies.

The pescatarian diet, when done right, is a holistic approach to help tackle your weight-loss goals. I've created the following pillars that will set you on the path to meaningful lifestyle changes:

1. **Respect Your Body.** Fuel your body with the nutrients it needs to thrive. Listen to what your body tells you it wants, instead of being restrictive. Put to rest all the negative self-talk, like "I look fat," "I need to lose a few pounds," or "I shouldn't have eaten that." These are destructive and inhibiting. Your body is a gift and a power-house, so treat it and talk to it like one.

2. **Move Your Body.** Our bodies are designed to move. Find movement that you love and that is easy for you to do almost every day, for the rest of your life. It can be as simple as walking.

3. **Rest Your Body.** Our bodies are good at telling us when we are overdoing it. Neck pain from stress and back pain from lifting heavy items are painful by-products when we overexert ourselves. Rest and relaxation are fundamentals of self-care. Caring for yourself is the basis of being able to take care of others.

As I mentioned in the beginning of this book, the pescatarian diet it is more than just a diet; it's a lifestyle. A lifestyle takes into consideration all factors of one's well-being, including nutrition, exercise, stress reduction, and self-care. That's why it is so easy to be successful while engaging in it.

Setting Goals

Now it's time to make a plan! Changing behavior takes time, consistency, and commitment. When it comes to weight loss, healthier eating behaviors, exercise, or stress reduction, you will need to be strategic in your goal setting.

Goal Setting for Weight Loss: When it comes to weight loss, slow and steady is key! Although it's tempting to do something drastic and lose weight fast, this strategy never sticks. The healthiest way to lose weight and keep it off is to aim for 1 to 2 pounds a week.

Goal Setting for Healthier Eating Behaviors: Maybe you don't need to lose weight but your diet needs a total makeover, or perhaps you would like to change something small, such as drinking more water. Whatever it is, prioritize the things you want to change. Changing everything at once usually works only for a few weeks. Setting smaller goals and then building on those goals over time will set you up for long-term success.

Goal Setting for Exercise: You don't have to spend hours at a gym to fit in exercise. What you have to do is find a way to move your body in a way that you love, because it's something you need to do almost every day for the rest of your life. Get motivated and stay accountable by joining a walking group, recreation sports team, or exercise class.

Goal Setting for Rest and Relaxation: Never underestimate the importance of self-care. Set goals that will allow yourself time to rest and relax—listen to your body when it needs a break. Make it a goal to listen to your favorite music, a guided meditation, or a fun podcast, or treat yourself to a massage. At the end of the day, you are worth it, and taking care of your emotional and mental health is just as important as your physical health.

 GLUTEN FREE HEART-HEALTHY VEGETARIAN

 DAIRY-FREE LOW-CARB VEGAN

Breakfasts

Loaded Avocado Sweet Potato "Toast," page 42

Baked Egg and Smoked Salmon Stuffed Avocado

SERVES 4 / PREP TIME: 10 MINUTES / COOK TIME: 20 MINUTES

One of my favorite seasoning mixes for eggs is everything-bagel seasoning. This is all the delicious spices from an everything bagel but without the bagel—it tastes like heaven. This type of seasoning is becoming easier to find in local grocery stores. If your store doesn't carry it, you can always order it online or check out my tip below on how to make it at home.

2 ripe avocados
4 thinly sliced pieces
   smoked salmon
4 eggs
Freshly ground black pepper
1 tablespoon
   everything-bagel
   seasoning

1. Preheat the oven to 450°F. Line a baking sheet with parchment paper or aluminum foil.

2. Cut each avocado in half and take the pit out. Scoop out a small amount of avocado from each center, making more room for the filling. Place the avocado halves on the prepared baking sheet. Gently layer each avocado half with a piece of salmon, pressing the salmon so there is still a depression where the pit used to be.

3. In a small bowl, crack 1 egg. Transfer the yolk and as much white as fits to the center of the avocado half (I always have to use a tad bit less than the whole white). Repeat with the remaining 3 eggs and avocado halves. Sprinkle with black pepper to taste.

4. Bake for 15 to 20 minutes, or until the egg is set. Add a few shakes of everything-bagel seasoning to each avocado and devour!

Substitution tip: If you can't find everything-bagel seasoning, you can simply make it yourself with spices that you probably already have in your pantry. Just combine 2 tablespoons poppy seeds, 2 tablespoons sesame seeds, 1 tablespoon dried garlic, 1 tablespoon dried onion, and 2 teaspoons coarse sea salt. in a small bowl, mix well, and store in a sealed container.

Always check ingredient packaging for gluten-free labeling.

PER SERVING: Calories: 257; Total Fat: 20g; Saturated Fat: 4g; Omega-3 Fat: 258mg; Cholesterol: 173mg; Sodium: 402mg; Total Carbohydrates: 8g; Fiber: 5g; Sugars: 6g; Protein: 15g

Caprese Egg Muffin Cups

SERVES 4 / PREP TIME: 10 MINUTES / COOK TIME: 25 MINUTES

These egg "muffins" are the perfect grab-and-go breakfast for your busiest mornings—which is every morning at my house! When I make a batch over the weekend, they last the entire week, which makes my mornings much easier and tastier.

10 large eggs
½ cup 1% milk
Kosher salt
Freshly ground black pepper
2 teaspoons Italian
    seasoning
1 cup diced tomatoes
½ cup shredded
    mozzarella cheese
½ cup roughly chopped
    fresh basil, lightly packed
Cooking spray

1. Preheat the oven to 350°F.

2. Whisk together the eggs and milk in a bowl. Season with salt, black pepper, and the Italian seasoning. Add the tomatoes, mozzarella cheese, and basil to the bowl. Stir until it's all well combined.

3. Coat a 12-cup muffin tin with cooking spray. Fill the muffin cups halfway with the egg mixture.

4. Bake for 20 to 25 minutes, until the centers are set and no longer runny. Allow to cool slightly before serving.

Leftovers: Store in the refrigerator for up to 5 days and simply reheat in the microwave before enjoying. These egg muffins are also freezer-friendly. Make an extra batch, let cool, and individually wrap in aluminum foil. When you're looking for a quick breakfast, defrost in the microwave before rushing out the door.

PER SERVING (3 MUFFINS): Calories: 218; Total Fat: 14g; Saturated Fat: 5g; Omega-3 Fat: 161mg; Cholesterol: 470mg; Sodium: 251mg; Total Carbohydrates: 5g; Fiber: 1g; Sugars: 1g; Protein: 18g

Smoked Whitefish Bagel Chips

SERVES 4 / PREP TIME: 15 MINUTES

You can make this breakfast in no time without turning on your oven. This is a healthier version of a whitefish salad that pairs perfectly with a crunchy bagel chip. It's time to get crunching!

1 ripe avocado, pitted
  and peeled
¼ cup 2% plain Greek yogurt
Juice from 2 lemons
½ teaspoon grated
  lemon zest
1 pound smoked whitefish,
  boned and skinned
1 celery stalk, finely diced
¼ small red onion,
  finely diced
Sea salt
Freshly ground black pepper
12 (4-inch) round bagel chips
2 small radishes, thinly
  sliced (optional)
½ cup alfalfa sprouts
  (optional)

1. In a medium bowl, mash the avocado. Add the Greek yogurt, lemon juice, and lemon zest. Add the whitefish, celery, and red onion. Season with sea salt and black pepper. Using a wooden spoon, break up the whitefish and stir to combine.

2. Scoop a few spoonfuls of the whitefish salad onto each bagel chip. Garnish each chip with 2 or 3 radish slices and a pinch of alfalfa sprouts, if you desire. Serve right away.

Ingredient tip: Using bagel chips instead of a bagel gives you the same taste but with far fewer carbohydrates and calories than the entire bagel. Check out your local bagel store to see if they make bagel chips with their leftover bagels.

PER SERVING: Calories: 348; Total Fat: 24g; Saturated Fat: 4g; Omega-3 Fat: 281mg; Cholesterol: 29mg; Sodium: 450mg; Total Carbohydrates: 25g; Fiber: 3g; Sugars: 4g; Protein: 11g

Tomato and Herb Baked Ricotta Toast

SERVES 6 / PREP TIME: 5 MINUTES / COOK TIME: 15 MINUTES

The combination of herbs in the ricotta makes for a unique, fragrant piece of delicious toast. This breakfast is a crowd-pleaser in my home.

2 tablespoons olive oil, divided

1 tablespoon red wine vinegar

1 garlic clove, minced

1 pint cherry tomatoes, halved

Sea salt

Freshly ground black pepper

1 (8-ounce) container whole-milk ricotta cheese

¼ cup coarsely chopped fresh basil

¼ cup coarsely chopped fresh parsley

2 tablespoons finely chopped fresh oregano

1 tablespoon finely chopped fresh rosemary

6 (¾-inch-thick) slices sourdough bread

1. Preheat the oven to 400°F.

2. In a medium bowl, whisk together 1 tablespoon of oil and the red wine vinegar. Add the garlic and cherry tomatoes, and season with salt and black pepper. Mix until combined and set aside.

3. In another medium bowl, combine the ricotta, basil, parsley, oregano, and rosemary.

4. Line up the sourdough slices on a baking sheet. Brush each side of the bread with the remaining 1 tablespoon of olive oil. Scoop some of the herbed ricotta on top of each slice of bread. Top with the tomato mixture, pressing down so the tomatoes sink into the ricotta. Bake for 10 to 15 minutes, or until the tomatoes begin to blister and the cheese is golden.

Ingredient tip: I love using fresh herbs for this recipe straight from my garden pots during the summer. When my herbs aren't in bloom, dried herbs never disappointment.

PER SERVING: Calories: 204; Total Fat: 9g; Saturated Fat: 3g; Omega-3 Fat: 106mg; Cholesterol: 12mg; Sodium: 260mg; Total Carbohydrates: 24g; Fiber: 1g; Sugars: 3g; Protein: 9g

Loaded Avocado Sweet Potato "Toast"

SERVES 4 / PREP TIME: 5 MINUTES / COOK TIME: 15 MINUTES

This is basically a sweeter, lower-carb version of your traditional avocado toast. There is actually no bread involved in this recipe at all—our "toast" comes from the sweet potato. Give it a try and you'll see what I mean!

1 avocado, pitted and peeled
Sea salt
Freshly ground black pepper
1 large sweet potato, scrubbed with skin on and cut lengthwise into 4 slices
4 eggs
1 teaspoon thyme, for garnish
Pinch red pepper flakes

1. In a small bowl, mash the avocado and season with salt and black pepper. Set aside.

2. Turn the toaster on high. In batches, place the slices of sweet potato in the toaster. Keep toasting each slice until the sweet potato gets soft, slightly caramelized, and crispy along the edge.

3. Prepare the eggs whichever way you desire: hard-boiled, scrambled, poached, over easy, or sunny-side up.

4. Transfer each sweet potato slice to a plate. Top each slice with a quarter of the mashed avocado and 1 egg. Sprinkle with salt, black pepper, thyme, and the red pepper flakes.

Serving tip: If using an oven or toaster oven, preheat it to 375°F. Place the sweet potato slices on a baking sheet lined with aluminum foil or parchment paper. Bake for 15 to 20 minutes, turning once halfway. This recipe calls for a pinch of red pepper flakes, but you can always add your favorite spices on top—like the everything-bagel seasoning I mentioned in the recipe for Baked Egg and Smoked Salmon Stuffed Avocado (page 38).

PER SERVING: Calories: 163; Total Fat: 11g; Saturated Fat: 3g; Omega-3 Fat: 75mg; Cholesterol: 164mg; Sodium: 141mg; Total Carbohydrates: 11g; Fiber: 3g; Sugars: 4g; Protein: 7g

Creamy Slow-Cooked Apple Cinnamon Oatmeal

SERVES 4 TO 6 / PREP TIME: 10 MINUTES / COOK TIME: 3 TO 4 HOURS ON HIGH;
6 TO 8 HOURS ON LOW

Waking up to the smell of these warm cinnamon oats in the slow cooker will instantly put you in a good mood. The addition of Greek yogurt at the end makes these oats even creamier and also helps pack in protein for extra fullness. Don't worry if you don't have a slow cooker—these can be cooked on the stove top, too.

1 apple, peeled, cored, and chopped

1 tablespoon ground cinnamon, plus more for serving

1 teaspoon nutmeg

2 teaspoons vanilla extract

1 cup steel-cut oats

½ cup cinnamon applesauce

3 cups 1% milk

6 ounces 2% vanilla or plain Greek yogurt

½ cup walnuts, crushed

1. Put the apple, cinnamon, nutmeg, vanilla, steel-cut oats, applesauce, and milk in a slow cooker. Close and secure the lid. Cook on low for 6 to 8 hours or on high 3 to 4 hours. If you don't have a slow cooker, in a large saucepan, bring the milk to a soft boil over medium heat. Reduce to a simmer and add the apple, cinnamon, nutmeg, vanilla, oats, and applesauce. Cover and cook for 10 to 12 minutes, stirring occasionally. Turn off the heat, keeping the oats covered for another 2 to 3 minutes.

2. To serve, portion the oats into individual bowls and add a few spoonfuls of Greek yogurt to each bowl. Stir it in until creamy and smooth. Sprinkle each serving with about 2 tablespoons walnuts and a dash of cinnamon. Serve warm.

Substitution tip: Apple butter is easy to find in the fall and is usually available next to the jellies in the grocery store. It can be substituted for the applesauce to give the oatmeal a richer flavor.

Always check ingredient packaging for gluten-free labeling.

PER SERVING: Calories: 275; Total Fat: 8g; Saturated Fat: 3g; Omega-3 Fat: 926mg; Cholesterol: 16mg; Sodium: 128mg; Total Carbohydrates: 35g; Fiber: 6g; Sugars: 24g; Protein: 16g

Smoked Trout with Caper Cream Cheese

SERVES 4 / PREP TIME: 15 MINUTES

If you're looking for a fancy and quick brunch idea, look no further than this recipe. Trout is different and delicious, and it keeps my brunch menu fun and interesting.

4 slices thick, hearty
  whole-grain bread
4 ounces cream cheese
1 tablespoon chopped
  fresh chives, plus more
  for garnish
1 tablespoon freshly
  squeezed lemon juice
½ tablespoon capers
1 teaspoon grated lemon zest
Kosher salt
Freshly ground black pepper
2 (3.8-ounce) cans skinless,
  boneless smoked
  trout, drained
1 radish, thinly sliced
Olive oil, for garnish

1. Toast the bread in the toaster, toaster oven, or oven.

2. In a medium bowl, mix together the cream cheese, 1 tablespoon of chives, lemon juice, capers, and lemon zest. Season with salt and black pepper.

3. Once the bread is toasted, spread the cream cheese mixture onto each slice.

4. Divide the trout among the pieces of toast and garnish with the remaining chives and radish slices.

5. Top each slice with a drizzle of olive oil and serve right away.

Ingredient tip: The canned trout from my local grocery store is 3.8 ounces, packed in oil. After it is drained, it shrinks to 2.7 ounces—I know this because it says so on the label. To make sure you have just enough to make the recipe, take note of the serving size and nutrition label to determine the amount of trout when drained of oil.

PER SERVING: Calories: 230; Total Fat: 15g; Saturated Fat: 7g; Omega-3 Fat: 215mg; Cholesterol: 53mg; Sodium: 550mg; Total Carbohydrates: 14g; Fiber: 2g; Sugars: 2g; Protein: 13g

Rise-and-Shine Green Smoothie Bowl

SERVES 2 / PREP TIME: 5 MINUTES / COOK TIME: 5 MINUTES

Yes, chewing your smoothie is a thing! Sometimes when we drink our calories, we don't get the same sensation of fullness as when we eat them. Eating your smoothie with a spoon and adding some crunchy seeds or nuts or chunks of fruit will help you slow down, fill up, and enjoy your smoothie a little bit longer.

¾ cup frozen
   pineapple chunks
¾ cup frozen mango chunks
½ banana
6 ounces 2% plain
   Greek yogurt
1½ cups 1% milk
2 handfuls ice cubes
2 teaspoons honey
2 cups spinach

Recommended toppings
Chia seeds
Sliced almonds
Sliced banana
Pineapple or mango chunks
Unsweetened coconut flakes

1. Place the pineapple chunks, mango chunks, banana, Greek yogurt, milk, ice, honey, and spinach in a blender. Blend until smooth and creamy. Pour the smoothie into 2 bowls, dividing the contents equally.

2. Decorate each bowl with the recommended toppings of choice.

3. Chew away!

Ingredient tip: I typically use frozen fruit for smoothies—I find frozen produce easier (no washing or cutting), and it also makes the smoothie colder, which I find more refreshing. There is basically no difference in the nutritional value between fresh and frozen fruit. The fruit is picked when ripe, then frozen soon after. Fresh versus frozen? The choice is yours!

Always check ingredient packaging for gluten-free labeling.

PER SERVING: Calories: 292; Total Fat: 4g; Saturated Fat: 2g; Omega-3 Fat: 128mg; Cholesterol: 18mg; Sodium: 122mg; Total Carbohydrates: 53g; Fiber: 3g; Sugars: 46g; Protein: 15g

5

Soups and Salads

Baked Salmon Salad with Strawberry and
Lemon Poppy Seed Dressing, page 64

Corn Bisque with Smoked Chili Oil and Crab

SERVES 4 / PREP TIME: 10 MINUTES / COOK TIME: 40 MINUTES

The complex combination of flavors in this bisque will wow your taste buds! I love the combination of the sweet corn with the spicy chili oil, and you will, too. Every time I make this soup, I feel like a real-deal chef at a fancy restaurant. I like feeling accomplished and proud after making this super yummy bisque.

6 tablespoons olive
oil, divided

1 yellow onion, diced

½ teaspoon kosher salt, plus
more for seasoning

3 garlic cloves, chopped

2 thyme sprigs

1 bay leaf

1 (16-ounce) bag frozen corn
kernels, thawed

3 cups reduced-sodium
vegetable stock

1 tablespoon
smoked paprika

½ teaspoon red
pepper flakes

¼ teaspoon chipotle powder

1 (6-ounce) can pasteurized
crabmeat

1 tablespoon minced
fresh chives

Freshly ground black pepper

1. In a large soup pot, heat 1 tablespoon of olive oil over medium heat. Add the onion and salt, and cook for 3 to 4 minutes, until the onion is translucent. Add the garlic, thyme, and bay leaf. Cook for an additional 2 minutes, then add the corn kernels and vegetable stock. Bring to a simmer and cook for 30 minutes.

2. While the soup is simmering, make the chili oil. In a small saucepan over medium heat, whisk together 3 tablespoons of olive oil with the smoked paprika, red pepper flakes, and chipotle powder for 3 to 4 minutes, or until a thermometer inserted into the oil reaches 250°F. Let the oil cool for 20 minutes. Strain through a coffee filter and set aside.

3. Remove the bay leaf and thyme. In batches, transfer the soup to a blender. Blend on high until smooth. Transfer the contents back into the soup pot, adjust the seasoning with salt and pepper, and reheat until warm.

4. In a small mixing bowl, add the crabmeat, the remaining 2 tablespoons of olive oil, and chives. Season with salt and pepper. Mix thoroughly.

5. To serve, ladle the soup evenly into 4 bowls. Place 2 ounces crabmeat in the center of each bowl. Drizzle ½ teaspoon (or more if you like it very spicy) smoked chili oil around the crab. Serve warm or chilled.

Substitution tip: Depending on where you live, it may be just as easy to find fresh crabmeat as it is to find canned. Where I live on the East Coast, fresh crabmeat is readily available in my local grocery store. Use whichever variety suits your preference.

Always check ingredient packaging for gluten-free labeling.

PER SERVING: Calories: 348; Total Fat: 23g; Saturated Fat: 3g; Omega-3 Fat: 302mg; Cholesterol: 49mg; Sodium: 580mg; Total Carbohydrates: 29g; Fiber: 3g; Sugars: 7g; Protein: 14g

Peach-Melon Gazpacho with Grilled Shrimp

SERVES 6 / PREP TIME: 15 MINUTES, PLUS 20 MINUTES
TO MARINATE / COOK TIME: 25 MINUTES

Summer is my favorite season not only because of the weather but also because of the produce. There is nothing better than perfectly ripened fruits on a hot summer day. This soup combines summer's freshest produce, perfectly chilled, with deliciously marinated grilled shrimp. I like to enjoy this soup as an appetizer or as a light summer dinner paired with a simple tossed salad.

3 cups cubed ripe cantaloupe

1 cup diced ripe peaches

1 tablespoon minced shallots

1 tablespoon freshly
   squeezed lemon juice

1 tablespoon rice wine
   vinegar

1 teaspoon kosher
   salt, divided

¼ teaspoon freshly ground
   black pepper

⅓ cup water

2 tablespoons chopped
   lemongrass

1 garlic clove

½ teaspoon minced
   fresh ginger

1 tablespoon olive oil, plus
   more for garnish

⅛ teaspoon red
   pepper flakes

12 medium shrimp, peeled
   and deveined

Vegetable oil, for oiling
   grill grates

1 tablespoon chiffonade
   of mint

1. Combine the cantaloupe, peaches, shallots, lemon juice, rice wine vinegar, ½ teaspoon of salt, black pepper, and water in a blender. Purée on high until smooth. Cover and reserve in the refrigerator.

2. In a food processor, purée the lemongrass, garlic, ginger, olive oil, red pepper flakes, and remaining ½ teaspoon of salt to a fine paste.

3. In a mixing bowl, toss the shrimp with the lemongrass paste and marinate for 20 minutes in the refrigerator.

4. Preheat the grill to high. Make sure the grill grates are clean, then oil them with vegetable oil. Grill the shrimp over high heat for 1 to 2 minutes on each side. Remove and chill.

5. Divide the soup among 6 bowls and top with 2 shrimp each. Garnish with the mint chiffonade and a drizzle of olive oil.

Ingredient tip: I love using lemongrass for soups, marinades, salads, and stir-fries. My local grocery store sells ready-to-use lemongrass pieces in the produce section, and my local Asian market sells long lemongrass stalks. When using the stalks, chop off about 2 inches from the root end and all of the leafy parts from the other end. You will end up with 4 to 5 inches of lemongrass once both ends are chopped off. Before cooking, peel off the outer layer, which tends to be dry and fibrous.

Always check ingredient packaging for gluten-free labeling.

PER SERVING: Calories: 267; Total Fat: 12g; Saturated Fat: 1g; Omega-3 Fat: 136mg; Cholesterol: 221mg; Sodium: 856mg; Total Carbohydrates: 14g; Fiber: 2g; Sugars: 2g; Protein: 25g

Roasted Tomato and Basil Soup

SERVES 4 / PREP TIME: 10 MINUTES / COOK TIME: 50 MINUTES

I love using farm-fresh heirloom tomatoes for this recipe, but you can use your favorite kind. Where I am from in New Jersey, we are fortunate to have the best tomatoes, which are super abundant during the warmer months. When summer is ending and everyone is harvesting their last batch of tomatoes from their gardens, I round up the extras to make and freeze as many batches of this soup as possible so I can enjoy it while snuggled on the couch all winter long.

8 ripe heirloom tomatoes, diced

5 tablespoons olive oil, divided, plus more for garnish

Kosher salt

Freshly ground black pepper

4 garlic cloves, smashed

1 shallot, chopped

1 teaspoon fennel seeds

4 cups reduced-sodium vegetable stock

1 cup thinly sliced fresh basil, divided

1. Preheat the oven to 450°F. Line a baking sheet with aluminum foil.

2. Place the tomatoes on the prepared baking sheet and toss them with 1 tablespoon of olive oil and salt and black pepper to taste. Roast for 20 minutes.

3. Once the tomatoes are done roasting, add 2 tablespoons of olive oil and the garlic, shallot, and fennel seeds to a large pot. Cook over medium heat for 3 to 4 minutes. Add the roasted tomatoes with all their drippings from the baking sheet. Add the stock and ½ cup of basil. Simmer for 30 minutes. Let cool.

4. In batches, transfer the mixture to a blender and purée at high speed. While blending, drizzle in the remaining 2 tablespoons of olive oil.

5. Serve the soup either hot or chilled. Garnish with the remaining ½ cup of basil and drizzle with olive oil, if desired.

Variation tip: If you choose to serve this soup cold, I would recommend chilling it overnight in the refrigerator, which allows all the flavors to settle. If you choose to freeze this soup, do so in a plastic container or a quart-size plastic bag. Before freezing, let the soup cool. Be sure to label the container or bag with the date it was made. Freeze for up to 4 months. When ready to use, thaw in the refrigerator for 1 to 2 days, or heat the soup while it's still frozen over low heat on the stove top.

Always check ingredient packaging for gluten-free labeling.

PER SERVING: Calories: 235; Total Fat: 20g; Saturated Fat: 5g; Omega-3 Fat: mg; Cholesterol: 0mg; Sodium: 778mg; Total Carbohydrates: 18g; Fiber: 5g; Sugars: 12g; Protein: 4g

Quinoa Miso Broth Bowl with Cod

SERVES 4 / PREP TIME: 10 MINUTES / COOK TIME: 20 MINUTES

Miso is a high-protein food paste made from fermented soybeans. It brings the savory taste of umami to the table, and the fermentation process creates gut-friendly probiotics, which are key players for healthy digestion and even immunity.

4 (3-ounce) cod fillets
Kosher salt
Freshly ground black pepper
1 tablespoon coconut oil
2 stalks lemongrass (each
    about 4 inches long),
    thinly sliced
1 shallot, finely chopped
2 teaspoons minced
    fresh ginger
2 garlic cloves, minced
8 cups reduced-sodium
    vegetable stock
Juice of 2 lemons
½ cup quinoa, rinsed
1 tablespoon miso paste
1 cup shredded carrots
2 handfuls snow peas
1 pound fresh spinach
1 cup chopped fresh cilantro
1 lemon, cut into rounds

1. Season the cod fillets with salt and black pepper. Set aside.

2. Heat the coconut oil in a large soup pot over medium heat. Add the lemongrass, shallot, ginger, and garlic. Cook for 2 to 3 minutes. Add the vegetable stock and lemon juice. Bring to a boil.

3. Once boiling, add the quinoa and reduce to a simmer. Let cook for another 10 minutes.

4. Spoon the miso into a small bowl, add a few tablespoons of hot water, and whisk until smooth. Stir the mixture into the soup.

5. When the soup comes back up to a simmer, add the cod fillets, carrots, and snow peas. Simmer for another 5 to 7 minutes, until the fish is cooked but not overcooked.

6. To serve, put a heaping handful of spinach in each of 4 soup bowls. Gently scooping the fish out of the pot, place a fillet in each bowl. Using a ladle, divide the broth evenly among the bowls. Garnish with the cilantro and lemon rounds.

Ingredient tip: As you may have noticed, the quinoa cooks directly in the broth of the soup, which is super convenient and saves a pot. Make sure to rinse the quinoa first—this removes the natural outer compound that makes it taste bitter. Check the package; some brands will let you know that it's already been rinsed.

PER SERVING: Calories: 306; Total Fat: 6g; Saturated Fat: 3g; Omega-3 Fat: 384mg; Cholesterol: 41mg; Sodium: 432mg; Total Carbohydrates: 40g; Fiber: 9g; Sugars: 12g; Protein: 27g

Southwestern Butternut Squash Soup

SERVES 6 / PREP TIME: 10 MINUTES / COOK TIME: 30 MINUTES

I came up with this soup idea one night when I was hungry but couldn't exactly pinpoint what I was in the mood for. I had all the ingredients for a simple butternut squash soup, but I needed something more substantial for it to be satisfying. I had this crazy idea to make a tortilla soup with butternut squash as the base. Then I figured I'd throw in some quinoa for additional fiber and protein. And that, ladies and gents, is how this soup was born.

1 butternut squash, peeled and cubed (about 2½ cups)

1 yellow onion, cut into 8 pieces

2 tablespoons olive oil, divided

½ teaspoon kosher salt

½ teaspoon freshly ground black pepper

1 teaspoon ground cumin

½ teaspoon chili powder

6 cups reduced-sodium vegetable stock, divided

½ cup quinoa, rinsed

1 (15-ounce) can no-salt-added black beans, drained and rinsed

1 cup fresh or frozen corn kernels, thawed if frozen

2 teaspoons sriracha, plus more for garnish

½ to 1 jalapeño pepper (according to your spice preference), seeded and deveined

6 ounces 2% plain Greek yogurt

Lime wedges, for garnish

6 ounces tortilla chips, crushed

1. Preheat the oven to 375°F. Line a baking sheet with parchment paper or aluminum foil.

2. Put the butternut squash and onion on the prepared baking sheet. Drizzle with 1 tablespoon of oil and toss until the vegetables are evenly coated. Season with the salt, black pepper, cumin, and chili powder. Bake for 25 to 30 minutes.

3. Meanwhile, in a large soup pot, bring 4 cups of vegetable stock to a boil. Add the quinoa and simmer for 10 minutes. Add the black beans and corn kernels. Reduce the heat to low.

4. Once the butternut squash and onion are finished baking, carefully transfer them to a blender. Add the sriracha, jalapeño pepper, and remaining 2 cups of vegetable stock to the blender. Blend on high until smooth. Depending on the size of your blender, you may have to blend in batches. ➤

5. Transfer the butternut squash mixture to the soup pot. Stir until evenly combined.

6. To serve, divide the soup among bowls and garnish each with a drizzle of sriracha, a dollop of yogurt, a lime wedge, and a small handful of crushed tortilla chips.

Ingredient tip: Save time by buying precut butternut squash from the produce section of your local grocery store.

Always check ingredient packaging for gluten-free labeling.

PER SERVING: Calories: 322; Total Fat: 8g; Saturated Fat: 1g; Omega-3 Fat: 140mg; Cholesterol: 3mg; Sodium: 432mg; Total Carbohydrates: 57g; Fiber: 9g; Sugars: 7g; Protein: 11g

Freekeh Salad with Arugula and Peaches

SERVES 4 / PREP TIME: 10 MINUTES / COOK TIME: 20 MINUTES

I could eat salads every day—and most weeks I do! I see how it can be easy to get into a rut with salads by using the same leafy greens, toppings, and dressing. I keep my salads exciting by using different whole grains, which changes the flavor and texture, and by adding fruit, which gives the salad a unique touch of sweetness.

1¼ cups water
⅛ teaspoon sea salt, plus ¼ teaspoon
½ cup freekeh
2 tablespoons champagne vinegar
3 tablespoons olive oil
2 teaspoons honey
1 tablespoon freshly squeezed lemon juice
Freshly ground black pepper
5 ounces arugula
2 ripe peaches, pitted and sliced
¼ cup slivered almonds
⅓ cup Pecorino Romano, cut into slivers

1. In a medium saucepan, bring the water and ⅛ teaspoon of salt to a boil. Add the freekeh, cover, and reduce heat to medium-low. Simmer for 15 minutes, or until the liquid is absorbed.

2. In a small mixing bowl, whisk together the champagne vinegar, olive oil, honey, lemon juice, black pepper to taste, and remaining ¼ teaspoon of sea salt.

3. Place the arugula, peaches, and cooked freekeh in a large serving bowl. Drizzle with the dressing and toss gently. Add the almonds and Pecorino Romano just before serving.

Ingredient tip: Half a cup of uncooked freekeh makes about 1.5 cups cooked. What is freekeh anyway? Freekeh is wheat that's harvested while young and then roasted. It's loaded with fiber and protein, perfect for anyone who enjoys feeling fuller for longer after a meal. Can't find freekeh? No problem. You can use any whole grain in this salad—barley or wheat berries are two great substitutes. If you are looking for a gluten-free substitute, use quinoa.

PER SERVING: Calories: 297; Total Fat: 18g; Saturated Fat: 4g; Omega-3 Fat: 113mg; Cholesterol: 11mg; Sodium: 393mg; Total Carbohydrates: 27g; Fiber: 4g; Sugars: 12g; Protein: 10g

Seared Tuna Salad with Wheat Berries and Wasabi Vinaigrette

SERVES 4 / PREP TIME: 15 MINUTES, PLUS 1 HOUR TO MARINATE / COOK TIME: 1 HOUR

When I started working in New York City, my bank statement basically became my food diary. I was eating out so much! I tried almost every restaurant within a mile radius of my job. I used to order this salad out on a weekly basis but then got frustrated when it was time to pay my credit card bill. I knew it was time to re-create this salad at home. I must say, this is a perfect, less expensive rendition of that salad I used to eat out all the time. It's healthier, too, because I control what I put in.

For the tuna steaks

2 tablespoons sesame oil

1 tablespoon
reduced-sodium soy sauce

1 tablespoon minced
fresh ginger

1 garlic clove, minced

2 (8-ounce) ahi tuna steaks
(1½ inches thick)

1 tablespoon canola oil

For the wheat berries

½ cup wheat berries

1¾ cups water

Kosher salt

TO MAKE THE TUNA STEAKS

1. Marinate the tuna steaks: In a medium bowl, whisk together the sesame oil, soy sauce, ginger, and garlic. Using a paper towel, pat the tuna steaks dry, and place them in a glass or ceramic dish. Pour the marinade over the tuna steaks. Cover tightly and let sit in the refrigerator for at least 1 hour or up to 8 hours. Flip the tuna once while marinating.

2. Heat the canola oil in a cast-iron or nonstick skillet over high heat. Once the oil is hot, sear the tuna steaks for 1 minute, 30 seconds on each side, or longer if you like yours less rare. (If your steaks are less than 1-inch thick, sear for 45 seconds on each side.) Remove the tuna from the pan and slice crosswise into ¼-inch-thick slices.

TO MAKE THE WHEAT BERRIES

In a saucepan, combine the wheat berries, water, and salt to taste. Bring to a boil, reduce heat, cover, and simmer for 1 hour, or until tender. Once done, drain any excess water and set aside.

For the vinaigrette

1 tablespoon sesame oil

1 tablespoon olive oil

2 teaspoons wasabi paste
(Japanese horseradish)

1 tablespoon rice wine
vinegar

1 tablespoon freshly
squeezed lime juice

1 teaspoon reduced-sodium
soy sauce

1 teaspoon minced
fresh ginger

For the salad

6 ounces arugula

1 cup edamame, shelled,
and thawed if frozen

½ red onion, sliced into
half-moons

TO MAKE THE VINAIGRETTE

Whisk the sesame oil, olive oil, wasabi, vinegar, lime juice, soy sauce, and ginger together and set aside.

TO MAKE THE SALAD

1. Place the arugula, edamame, and red onion in a salad bowl. Drizzle on the wasabi vinaigrette and gently toss.

2. To serve, divide the tossed salad among 4 bowls or plates and top with the tuna and wheat berries. Serve and enjoy.

Ingredient tip: Wheat berries remind me of little popcorn kernels. They take a full hour to cook, but don't be put off by the long cooking time, because they're incredibly easy to prepare. Even if you add too much liquid, they soak up what they need and you can drain off the excess. I love wheat berries because they are super chewy, nutty, and high in both protein and fiber.

PER SERVING: Calories: 418; Total Fat: 23g; Saturated Fat: 3g; Omega-3 Fat: 1597mg; Cholesterol: 50mg; Sodium: 240mg; Total Carbohydrates: 17g; Fiber: 5g; Sugars: 2g; Protein: 36g

Citrusy Endive Salad with Toasted Pistachios

SERVES 4 TO 6 / PREP TIME: 10 MINUTES / COOK TIME: 10 MINUTES

This showstopping endive dish will look like a work of art at the center of your table. This is definitely not your traditional salad. I love giving endive the attention it deserves, while pairing it with sweet mandarin oranges, creamy goat cheese, and fragrant toasted pistachios.

⅓ cup pistachios, shelled
1 (10.5-ounce) can mandarin
   oranges packed in
   100% juice
3 tablespoons olive oil
Juice of ½ lime
⅛ teaspoon kosher salt
Freshly ground black pepper
2 heads endive,
   roughly chopped
4 cups baby spinach
¼ onion, thinly sliced
⅓ cup crumbled goat cheese

1. Preheat oven to 400°F. Line a baking sheet with parchment paper or aluminum foil.

2. Spread the pistachios on the prepared baking sheet. Bake for 7 to 8 minutes, rotating halfway through, until the nuts are fragrant. Set aside to cool.

3. Drain the mandarin oranges, reserving 3 tablespoons of juice to make the dressing. Place the oranges in a bowl and set aside.

4. In a mixing bowl, whisk together the reserved mandarin orange juice, olive oil, lime juice, salt, and black pepper to taste. Set aside.

5. In a large salad bowl, place the endive, spinach, onion, toasted pistachios, and mandarin oranges. Drizzle the dressing over the salad. Toss gently until evenly coated.

6. Add the crumbled goat cheese over the top and serve.

Ingredient tip: When purchasing canned fruit, I always look for fruit packed in 100% fruit juice, which is tremendously lower in sugar than fruit packed in light or heavy syrup. For this recipe, I reserve some of the juice to make the dressing, which really boosts the flavor by adding some natural sweetness. You can freeze the juice from canned fruit in ice cube trays. The juice can last up to 4 to 6 months in the freezer and makes for great additions to marinades, sauces, and dressings.

PER SERVING: Calories: 243; Total Fat: 17g; Saturated Fat: 5g; Omega-3 Fat: 197mg; Cholesterol: 11mg; Sodium: 527mg; Total Carbohydrates: 18g; Fiber: 8g; Sugars: 6g; Protein: 9g

Watermelon and Avocado Salad with Tomatoes, Roasted Corn, and Fresh Herbs

SERVES 4 TO 6 / PREP TIME: 15 MINUTES, PLUS
30 MINUTES TO MARINATE / COOK TIME: 10 MINUTES

This salad represents the bounty of summer in a bowl. It has all my favorite summer ingredients: juicy watermelon, sweet corn, creamy avocados, and, oh yes, farm-fresh herbs and tomatoes.

2 ears corn, shucked
3 tablespoons olive oil, divided
2 tablespoons balsamic vinegar
2 teaspoons honey
Kosher salt
4 cups cubed watermelon (1-inch cubes)
2 heirloom tomatoes, chopped
2 avocados, pitted, peeled, and chopped
½ cup roughly chopped fresh mint, lightly packed
½ cup roughly chopped fresh basil, lightly packed

1. Preheat the grill to medium-high heat or the oven to 400°F.

2. Coat both ears of corn with 1 tablespoon of olive oil. Grill for 7 to 10 minutes, or until the corn is lightly browned. Remove from the grill and let cool. Once cool, cut the kernels from the cob and transfer to a bowl. Set aside.

3. In a mixing bowl, whisk the remaining 2 tablespoons of olive oil, balsamic vinegar, honey, and salt to taste. Set aside.

4. Put the watermelon, tomatoes, avocados, mint, basil, and roasted corn in a large salad bowl. Drizzle with the dressing and gently toss until evenly coated.

5. Cover with plastic wrap and let marinate in the refrigerator for 30 minutes.

6. Serve cold.

Substitution tip: I love roasted corn, but during the winter, fresh corn is impossible to find and my grill is off-limits (mostly because I'm so intolerant to the cold). Of course, you can thaw frozen corn kernels, soak up moisture with a paper towel, and roast the corn in the oven for 15 to 20 minutes (tossing halfway through). A great shortcut is to buy frozen roasted corn, which my local grocery store began carrying a few years ago. It may not be exactly the same as fresh New Jersey corn, but it's close enough for me!

PER SERVING: Calories: 369; Total Fat: 25g; Saturated Fat: 4g; Omega-3 Fat: 96mg; Cholesterol: 0mg; Sodium: 63mg; Total Carbohydrates: 39g; Fiber: 8g; Sugars: 17g; Protein: 6g

Cajun Shrimp Salad with Mango-Peach Salsa

SERVES 4 / PREP TIME: 10 MINUTES, PLUS 30 MINUTES TO MARINATE / COOK TIME: 5 MINUTES

It doesn't get any simpler than this! I love using shrimp for salads because it marinates quickly and cooks even quicker. This mango-peach salsa is the perfect combination for this Cajun shrimp salad. It's so juicy and flavorful that it eliminates the need for dressing.

1 pound medium shrimp, peeled and deveined
1 tablespoon Cajun seasoning
Juice of 2 limes, divided
1 mango, pitted and cubed
2 peaches, pitted and chopped
½ red onion, diced
½ cup roughly chopped fresh cilantro
½ jalapeño pepper, seeded and finely chopped
Kosher salt
Freshly ground black pepper
1 pound baby spinach
2 teaspoons olive oil

1. In a large mixing bowl, place the shrimp, Cajun seasoning, and juice of 1 lime. Toss until the shrimp are fully coated. Marinate in the refrigerator for 30 minutes.

2. In another large bowl, mix the remaining lime juice, mango, peaches, red onion, cilantro, and jalapeño pepper, and season with salt and black pepper. Add the spinach and toss gently until everything is combined.

3. In a large skillet, heat the olive oil over medium heat. Once the oil is hot, add the shrimp to the pan in a single layer. Cook for 2 minutes, flip, and cook for another 1 to 2 minutes. Transfer the shrimp to the salad.

4. Evenly divide the salad among 4 plates and serve.

Ingredient tip: Make a double batch of this mango-peach salsa and store it in the refrigerator to use as a topping for fish throughout the week. I love using this salsa on top of both salmon and whitefish. As a plus, this salsa gets even tastier as the ingredients meld together. It keeps in the refrigerator for 4 to 5 days. Also, you can make your own Cajun seasoning at home. Simply mix together equal amounts of cumin, coriander, and paprika. Then add a pinch of salt and freshly ground pepper.

PER SERVING: Calories: 246; Total Fat: 5g; Saturated Fat: 1g; Omega-3 Fat: 783mg; Cholesterol: 223mg; Sodium: 425mg; Total Carbohydrates: 27g; Fiber: 6g; Sugars: 20g; Protein: 29g

Baked Salmon Salad with Strawberry and Lemon Poppy Seed Dressing

SERVES 4 / PREP TIME: 10 MINUTES / COOK TIME: 15 MINUTES

Pairing citrus and leafy green veggies has been a staple in my life ever since being diagnosed with iron-deficiency anemia while in college. For anyone who doesn't eat red meat, it's important to eat iron-rich plant foods, such as leafy green veggies. Pairing leafy greens with citrus helps boost the absorption of the iron. The best part is that these two foods naturally taste magnificent together.

For the salmon

4 (4-ounce) salmon fillets

2 teaspoons olive oil

2 tablespoons chopped fresh dill

4 tablespoons freshly squeezed lemon juice

⅛ teaspoon kosher salt

For the dressing

2 tablespoons champagne vinegar

2 tablespoons olive oil

2 teaspoons honey

1 tablespoon freshly squeezed lemon juice

1 tablespoon poppy seeds

½ shallot, finely chopped

½ teaspoon dried mustard

TO MAKE THE SALMON

1. Preheat the oven to 375°F. Line a baking sheet with aluminum foil or parchment paper.

2. Place the salmon fillets on the prepared baking sheet. In a glass measuring cup with a pour spout, whisk together the olive oil, dill, lemon juice, and salt. Pour the dressing evenly over each fillet. Bake for 12 to 15 minutes, or until the salmon flakes with a fork.

TO MAKE THE DRESSING

While the salmon is baking, make the dressing by combining the vinegar, olive oil, honey, lemon juice, poppy seeds, shallot, and mustard in a medium bowl. Mix until the poppy seeds are evenly distributed. Set aside.

For the salad

1 pound baby spinach

1 cup strawberries, trimmed
  and quartered

¼ cup crumbled feta cheese

¼ cup pine nuts

TO MAKE THE SALAD

1. Put the spinach and strawberries in a large bowl. Drizzle the dressing over and gently toss.

2. Divide the salad evenly among 4 bowls and sprinkle with the feta cheese and pine nuts. Top each salad with a salmon fillet.

Ingredient tip: I often make this salad for work. At night when I'm prepping for lunch the next day, which is usually right after dinner, I don't always feel like baking salmon. To replace the fresh salmon fillet, I'll used canned salmon. Just mix the oil, dill, lemon juice, and salt in a bowl with the canned salmon and top your salad with it.

PER SERVING: Calories: 435; Total Fat: 31g; Saturated Fat: 6g; Omega-3 Fat: 2511mg; Cholesterol: 73mg; Sodium: 342mg; Total Carbohydrates: 14g; Fiber: 4g; Sugars: 7g; Protein: 29g

Honey Barbeque Salmon Cobb Salad with Citrus Vinaigrette

SERVES 4 / PREP TIME: 15 MINUTES / COOK TIME: 15 MINUTES

This perfectly decorated salad gives the traditional Cobb salad a run for its money. The salmon fillets are deliciously marinated in a homemade barbecue sauce. When paired with the citrus-coated plant-based toppings, this salad is the perfect combination of protein, plants, and flavor!

For the salmon

4 (4-ounce) salmon fillets
½ cup ketchup
¼ cup honey
2 tablespoons apple cider vinegar
1 teaspoon Worcestershire sauce
1 garlic clove, minced
¼ teaspoon chili powder
¼ teaspoon ground cayenne pepper
Vegetable oil, for oiling grill grates

TO MAKE THE SALMON

1. Pat the salmon dry with a paper towel and place in a ceramic or glass dish.

2. Combine the ketchup, honey, apple cider vinegar, Worcestershire sauce, minced garlic, chili powder, and cayenne pepper in a small saucepan over medium heat. Whisk for 3 minutes and allow it to lightly bubble. Remove from heat and brush each salmon fillet with the sauce, making sure to coat both sides evenly.

3. Preheat the grill to medium-high heat. Brush the grill grates with vegetable oil.

4. Grill the salmon fillets for 8 to 10 minutes, flipping once. Transfer to a clean cutting board and let rest for 3 to 4 minutes.

For the dressing

3 tablespoons olive oil

3 tablespoons apple
cider vinegar

2 tablespoons freshly
squeezed lemon juice

2 tablespoons chopped
fresh cilantro, plus more
for garnish

1 tablespoon chopped fresh
dill, plus more for garnish

½ teaspoon grated
lemon zest

½ teaspoon freshly ground
black pepper

½ shallot, minced

Kosher salt

For the salad

4 eggs, hard-boiled, peeled,
and halved

1 head butter
lettuce, chopped

4 cups chopped
romaine lettuce

1 cup cored and diced
tomatoes

1 ripe avocado, pitted,
peeled, and diced

1 cup fresh or frozen corn
kernels, thawed if frozen

TO MAKE THE DRESSING

In a small bowl, whisk together the olive oil, vinegar, lemon juice, 2 tablespoons cilantro, 1 tablespoon dill, lemon zest, black pepper, shallot, and salt to taste. Set aside.

TO MAKE THE SALAD

In a serving dish, place the eggs, butter lettuce, romaine lettuce, tomatoes, avocado, and corn kernels. Drizzle the dressing over the salad and toss until evenly coated. Transfer the salmon fillets to the salad dish. Garnish with dill and cilantro and serve.

Ingredient tip: If you love this citrus vinaigrette as much as I do, then you may want to double or even triple this recipe and store the extra in the refrigerator for up to a week.

PER SERVING: Calories: 561; Total Fat: 32g; Saturated Fat: 6g; Omega-3 Fat: 2462mg; Cholesterol: 198mg; Sodium: 524mg; Total Carbohydrates: 43g; Fiber: 6g; Sugars: 29g; Protein: 27g

6
Vegetarian Mains

Caramelized Pear and Pomegranate
Salad Pizza, page 78

Spicy Tempeh Stir-Fry

SERVES 4 / PREP TIME: 10 MINUTES / COOK TIME: 15 MINUTES

Tempeh is one of the most versatile plant-based ingredients and often doesn't get the attention it deserves. Tempeh is high in both fiber and protein thanks to the fermented soybeans and whole grains. It's also great for gut health.

2 tablespoons peanut butter

2 tablespoons water

1 tablespoon sesame oil

1 tablespoon minced or grated fresh ginger

1 tablespoon sriracha (adjust the amount to your spice preference)

1 tablespoon reduced-sodium soy sauce

2 teaspoons honey

Juice of 1 lime

6 ounces tempeh, cut into 1-inch cubes

1 tablespoon olive oil

1 red onion, sliced

Kosher salt

Freshly ground black pepper

1 bunch asparagus, trimmed and halved crosswise

1 red bell pepper, seeded and sliced

1 cup snow peas

1 ounce peanuts, crushed

3 scallions, chopped

1. In a small bowl, whisk together the peanut butter, water, sesame oil, ginger, sriracha, soy sauce, honey, and lime juice.

2. In another bowl or dish, place the tempeh and pour half the sauce over it. Toss until fully coated. Set aside the other half of the sauce.

3. In a nonstick skillet over medium heat, add the olive oil. Once the oil is warm, add the red onion and season with salt and black pepper. Cook for 2 to 3 minutes. Add the asparagus, red bell pepper, and snow peas. Toss and cook until tender, 5 to 6 minutes. Once the vegetables are soft, add the remaining sauce to the skillet. Cook for another 3 minutes. Transfer the mixture to a dish and set aside.

4. Carefully wipe down the skillet. To the skillet, add the tempeh cubes, reserving the excess peanut sauce in the bowl. Cook each side of the tempeh for 3 minutes.

5. Add the vegetables back to the skillet. Drizzle the reserved sauce from the bowl into the pan and stir to combine.

6. To serve, divide the stir-fry among 4 plates or bowls and garnish with the peanuts and scallions.

Variation tip: Another one of my favorite ways to make this dish is to roast everything in the oven at 375°F. Make the sauce, then add half to the tempeh and transfer to a baking sheet lined with parchment paper or aluminum foil. Add the other half of the sauce to the veggies, toss, and transfer to another baking sheet lined with parchment paper or aluminum foil. Bake the tempeh for 10 minutes (flipping halfway through) and the veggies for 15 to 20 minutes. Combine everything in a large serving dish and enjoy over brown rice or warmed zucchini noodles.

PER SERVING: Calories: 298; Total Fat: 19g; Saturated Fat: 3g; Omega-3 Fat: 149mg; Cholesterol: 0mg; Sodium: 262mg; Total Carbohydrates: 22g; Fiber: 5g; Sugars: 10g; Protein: 15g

Chickpea and Sweet Potato Coconut Curry

SERVES 6 / PREP TIME: 10 MINUTES / COOK TIME: 30 MINUTES

I love making curries. They used to intimidate me because of all the spices—I was always afraid of adding too much or too little. What I've learned about making curry is that it is super quick because it requires only one pot. Veggie curries are even easier because they cook even faster. As far as spice goes, over time I became more confident in my seasoning skills. Tasting and adjusting the seasoning as you cook is key to a perfectly flavored curry.

2 tablespoons coconut oil
1 yellow onion, diced
Kosher salt
3 garlic cloves, minced
Freshly ground black pepper
2 celery stalks,
   finely chopped
2 large carrots,
   finely chopped
1 sweet potato, diced
2 tomatoes, cored and diced
2 tablespoons curry powder
½ teaspoon ground cumin
½ teaspoon paprika
2 (16-ounce) cans chickpeas,
   drained and rinsed
1 (13.5-ounce) can
   coconut cream
2 cups reduced-sodium
   vegetable stock
1 cup chopped fresh cilantro,
   lightly packed
Lime wedges, for garnish

1. In a large soup pot, heat the coconut oil over medium to high heat. Add the onion and season with salt. Cook for 2 to 3 minutes, until the onion is translucent.

2. Next, add the garlic, black pepper to taste, celery, carrots, sweet potato, tomatoes, curry powder, cumin, and paprika. Stir and let cook for 7 to 10 minutes.

3. Add the chickpeas, coconut cream, and vegetable stock. Simmer for 10 to 15 minutes, or until the sweet potato is soft.

4. Ladle the curry into a serving bowl and serve with the cilantro and lime wedges.

Leftovers: You can freeze this curry in a plastic container or quart-size resealable plastic bag. Before freezing, let the curry cool. Be sure to label the container or bag with the date it was made. Freeze for up to 4 months. When ready to use, thaw in the refrigerator for 1 to 2 days before heating, or heat the curry while it's still frozen over low heat on the stove top.

Always check ingredient packaging for gluten-free labeling.

PER SERVING: Calories: 410; Total Fat: 23g; Saturated Fat: 18g; Omega-3 Fat: 30mg; Cholesterol: 0mg; Sodium: 462mg; Total Carbohydrates: 48g; Fiber: 9; Sugars: 7g; Protein: 10g

Tex–Mex Tempeh Veggie Skillet

SERVES 6 / PREP TIME: 10 MINUTES / COOK TIME: 20 MINUTES

One-pot meals are a staple in my household. For me, cooking is therapeutic—I enjoy coming home from work and cooking a homemade dinner. What I don't enjoy is doing the dishes! This is a flavorful dish with easy cleanup that anyone could make in no time.

2 tablespoons olive
   oil, divided
1 red onion, diced
2 garlic cloves, minced
Kosher salt
Freshly ground black pepper
8 ounces tempeh, crumbled
1 teaspoon ground cumin
1 teaspoon dried oregano
1 (15-ounce) can no-salt-
   added black beans,
   drained and rinsed
1 (14.5-ounce) can
   fire-roasted tomatoes
1 cup fresh or frozen corn
   kernels, thawed if frozen
1 cup green beans, trimmed
   and cut in half
1 zucchini, diced
1 small red bell pepper,
   seeded and diced
1 cup shredded
   cheddar cheese
1 cup chopped fresh cilantro,
   lightly packed
Lime wedges, for garnish

1. Heat 1 tablespoon of olive oil in a large cast-iron skillet over medium-high heat. Add the red onion and garlic, and season with salt and black pepper. Cook for 2 to 3 minutes.

2. Add the tempeh, cumin, and oregano. Cook for another 3 minutes.

3. Add the remaining 1 tablespoon of oil. Add the black beans, tomatoes, corn, green beans, zucchini, and red bell pepper.

4. Toss to combine and cook for another 7 to 8 minutes. Adjust the seasoning to taste.

5. Add the cheese and cook until it is melted, 3 to 4 minutes.

6. Divide among 6 bowls. Garnish with the cilantro and lime wedges.

Substitution tip: Save time by seasoning this tempeh veggie skillet with your favorite low-sodium taco seasoning. Just be aware that low sodium and reduced sodium mean two very different things. Reduced sodium is 25 percent lower sodium than the original version. If the original version was super high in salt, the reduced-sodium version will still be high. You can't go wrong with buying products labeled low sodium, which means there is less than 140 mg of sodium per serving.

PER SERVING: Calories: 286; Total Fat: 16g; Saturated Fat: 6g; Omega-3 Fat: 239mg; Cholesterol: 20mg; Sodium: 176mg; Total Carbohydrates: 22g; Fiber: 5g; Sugars: 4g; Protein: 16g

Stove-Top Green Chili with Quinoa

SERVES 8 TO 10 / PREP TIME: 15 MINUTES / COOK TIME: 25 MINUTES

This chili was inspired by my daughter's love for salsa verde. She loves salsa verde so much that she eats it with a spoon. I decided to make this chili using her favorite salsa and I kept the color green in hopes of her actually trying a new dish during her picky-eating toddler years. My plan worked and we finally found a chili we both love.

1 tablespoon olive oil

1 yellow onion, chopped

Kosher salt

Freshly ground black pepper

2 garlic cloves, minced

1 (4-ounce) can green chiles

1 zucchini, peeled and diced

1 cup fresh or frozen corn kernels, thawed if frozen

4 cups reduced-sodium vegetable stock

¾ cup quinoa, rinsed

2 (14-ounce) cans no-salt-added white beans, such as cannellini or great northern beans, drained and rinsed

2 cups of your favorite store-bought salsa verde

2 teaspoons ground cumin

1 teaspoon dried oregano

Suggested toppings

Lime wedges

1 ripe avocado, diced

½ cup finely chopped fresh cilantro

½ cup shredded cheddar cheese

3 handfuls tortilla chips, crushed

1. In a large soup pot, heat the olive oil over medium heat. Add the onion and season with salt and black pepper. Cook until the onion is translucent, about 2 minutes. Add the garlic and cook for another minute. Add the green chiles, zucchini, and corn kernels. Cook until the zucchini is slightly soft.

2. Add the vegetable stock and bring to a boil. Once boiling, add the quinoa, lower to a simmer, cover, and cook for 10 minutes.

3. After 10 minutes, add the beans, salsa verde, cumin, and oregano. Cook uncovered for about 10 minutes, until it simmers again.

4. Serve in individual bowls with your favorite toppings.

Ingredient tip: This chili thickens as it cools. Add another ½ cup of stock if you find the consistency too thick after it's cooked or when you are reheating the leftovers. My favorite store-bought salsa verde is from Trader Joe's, but I've tried it with other brands that work as well. For this recipe, I love using frozen roasted corn, which is readily available in my local grocery store. I also love taking advantage of the 10 minutes while the quinoa cooks and doing some dishes. Time is never wasted in my kitchen! Last, this recipe makes a ton. It's super freezer-friendly. Freeze for up to 4 months.

Always check ingredient packaging for gluten-free labeling.

PER SERVING: Calories: 292; Total Fat: 5g; Saturated Fat: 1g; Omega-3 Fat: 188mg; Cholesterol: 0mg; Sodium: 356mg; Total Carbohydrates: 52g; Fiber: 12g; Sugars: 10g; Protein: 15g

Quinoa and Goat Cheese Stuffed Sweet Potato

SERVES 4 / PREP TIME: 15 MINUTES / COOK TIME: 1 HOUR

It doesn't get any easier than this recipe! The natural sweetness of the sweet potato paired with the creamy goat cheese is a match made in heaven.

4 sweet potatoes
Kosher salt
Freshly ground black pepper
¾ cup quinoa, rinsed
½ cup crumbled goat cheese
2 tablespoons honey
2 tablespoons chopped
   fresh rosemary

1. Preheat the oven to 400°F. Line a baking sheet with aluminum foil or parchment paper.

2. Pierce the sweet potatoes a few times with a fork. Season with salt and black pepper. Transfer to the prepared baking sheet and bake for 30 to 45 minutes, or until sweet potatoes are semisoft.

3. While the sweet potatoes are in the oven, cook the quinoa according to the package instructions.

4. In a medium mixing bowl, combine the goat cheese, honey, and rosemary, and season with salt and black pepper.

5. Once the quinoa is done cooking, fold it into the goat cheese mixture.

6. Remove the sweet potatoes from the oven but leave the oven on. When the sweet potatoes are cool enough, carefully cut each open lengthwise. Scoop out each sweet potato and stuff it with the quinoa and goat cheese mixture. Place back in the oven at 400°F for another 10 to 15 minutes, or until the cheese is gooey, golden, and slightly melted.

Ingredient tip: I like to make large amounts of quinoa on a weekly basis and use it in recipes throughout the week. Once it's cooked, you can throw it in soups, use it in a stir-fry, or toss it on a salad. Quinoa typically doubles after it's cooked, so when I plan on using it for the week, I'll make 2½ cups dried to get 5 cups cooked.

PER SERVING: Calories: 331; Total Fat: 7g; Saturated Fat: 4g; Omega-3 Fat: 99mg; Cholesterol: 15mg; Sodium: 162mg; Total Carbohydrates: 57g; Fiber: 6g; Sugars: 14g; Protein: 11g

Loaded Veggie Quesadillas

SERVES 4 / PREP TIME: 10 MINUTES / COOK TIME: 15 MINUTES

My daughter and I love quesadillas—they're super delicious and ready in no time. What sets these quesadillas apart from others is the filling fiber from all the veggies and black beans. You may have extra quesadilla filling, which I love using as a salad topper or just eating as is with a sprinkle of cheese.

1 tablespoon plus
   2 teaspoons olive
   oil, divided
1 zucchini, diced
1 small red bell
   pepper, diced
½ yellow onion, diced
⅛ teaspoon kosher salt
½ teaspoon freshly ground
   black pepper
½ teaspoon ground
   cayenne pepper
1 teaspoon chili powder
½ teaspoon ground cumin
1 (15-ounce) can no-salt-
   added black beans,
   drained and rinsed
½ cup fresh or frozen corn
   kernels, thawed if frozen
4 cups spinach
3 tablespoons chopped fresh
   cilantro
4 (6- to 8-inch) whole-wheat
   tortillas
1 cup shredded cheddar
   cheese, divided

1. Heat 1 tablespoon of oil in a large nonstick or cast-iron skillet over medium-high heat. Add the zucchini, red bell pepper, and onion. Cook until semisoft, 3 to 4 minutes.

2. Stir the mixture while adding the salt, black pepper, cayenne pepper, chili powder, and cumin. Then add the black beans and corn kernels. Cook for another 2 minutes.

3. Turn off the heat and add the spinach and cilantro. Transfer the mixture to a medium bowl and mix well.

4. Wipe down the skillet and add ½ teaspoon of oil to coat it over medium heat. Heat 1 tortilla for about 1 minute and then flip. Melt ¼ cup of cheese on top of the tortilla. Add ½ to ¾ cup veggie mixture to half of the tortilla, then fold the other half over the filling. Cook for 1 to 2 minutes per side, or until the quesadilla is golden brown, and transfer to a plate. Repeat with the remaining oil, tortillas, cheese, and filling, wiping down the skillet in between each quesadilla.

5. Cut each quesadilla into 2 wedges and serve while hot.

Ingredient tip: When shopping for tortillas, I always recommend 100% whole-wheat or 100% whole-grain tortillas that are between 6 and 8 inches across. I also look for tortillas that have minimal ingredients. I love the filling of this quesadilla so much that I often just skip the tortilla.

PER SERVING: Calories: 390; Total Fat: 19g; Saturated Fat: 7g; Omega-3 Fat: 305mg; Cholesterol: 30mg; Sodium: 849mg; Total Carbohydrates: 43g; Fiber: 13g; Sugars: 4g; Protein: 17g

Veggie Pad Thai with Tofu and Zucchini Ribbons

SERVES 4 / PREP TIME: 10 MINUTES / COOK TIME: 10 MINUTES

I absolutely love a good pad Thai. It's my go-to dish when I'm out for Thai food. I don't know about you, but after eating a large noodle-based dish, all I want to do is nap. No matter how many times I say I'll eat only half, it usually doesn't happen—it's just too good! When I decided to re-create this dish at home, it was a no-brainer that I needed to replace the noodles with zucchini ribbons. This easy swap really lightens up the dish while still soaking up all the traditional pad Thai flavors.

1 tablespoon olive oil, divided

1 small yellow onion, diced

3 zucchini, spiralized or cut into ribbons

1 cup shredded carrots

½ red bell pepper, seeded and thinly sliced

2 tablespoons sesame oil

1 tablespoon fish sauce

1 tablespoon rice wine vinegar

Juice of 1 lime

½ tablespoon reduced-sodium soy sauce

½ tablespoon honey

1 teaspoon chili paste

½ (14-ounce) package firm tofu, drained, patted dry, and cut into ½-inch cubes

2 eggs, scrambled

½ cup chopped fresh cilantro

⅓ cup peanuts, crushed

2 scallions, finely chopped

Lime wedges, for garnish

1. In a large skillet, heat ½ tablespoon of olive oil over medium heat. Add the onion and cook for 2 to 3 minutes, until translucent. Add the zucchini ribbons, carrots, and red bell pepper. Cook for 4 to 5 minutes, until soft.

2. While the zucchini ribbons are cooking, in a large bowl, mix the sesame oil, fish sauce, rice wine vinegar, lime juice, soy sauce, honey, and chili paste. Add the tofu to the bowl and toss until fully coated.

3. Add the tofu with all the sauce and the scrambled eggs to the skillet. Using tongs, toss the contents until the sauce coats the zucchini ribbons evenly.

4. Divide the pad Thai among 4 plates. Top each with a sprinkle of cilantro, peanuts, and scallions. Garnish with lime wedges and serve.

Ingredient tip: To make zucchini ribbons, use a spiralizer machine or a vegetable peeler. Or to save time, you can buy zucchini noodles premade from the produce department of your grocery store.

PER SERVING: Calories: 265; Total Fat: 20g; Saturated Fat: 3g; Omega-3 Fat: 86mg; Cholesterol: 82mg; Sodium: 506mg; Total Carbohydrates: 16g; Fiber: 4g; Sugars: 9g; Protein: 10g

Caramelized Pear and Pomegranate Salad Pizza

SERVES 4 / PREP TIME: 30 MINUTES, PLUS
45 MINUTES FOR THE DOUGH TO RISE / COOK TIME: 15 MINUTES

I'm sure by now you are well aware of my love for salads. Another way I keep salads interesting is by adding them to pizza. This dish is sweet, juicy, and crispy. I love the sweetness from the caramelized pears and the burst of juice from the pomegranate seeds.

For the honey wheat pizza dough

1 tablespoon active dry yeast

1½ cups warm water

2 cups whole-wheat flour

1½ cups all-purpose flour, plus more for dusting work surface

1 tablespoon olive oil

1 tablespoon honey

½ teaspoon kosher salt

For the pizza

2 tablespoons olive oil, divided

1 small sweet onion, chopped

2 teaspoons brown sugar

2 Seckel pears, seeded and thinly sliced, divided

4 cups arugula

2 tablespoons balsamic vinegar

Kosher salt

Freshly ground black pepper

¼ cup crumbled goat cheese

⅓ cup pomegranate seeds

TO MAKE THE HONEY WHEAT PIZZA DOUGH

1. In a measuring cup, proof the yeast by dissolving it in the water.

2. In a large bowl, add the whole-wheat flour and all-purpose flour. Make a well in the center and add the proofed yeast, olive oil, honey, and salt. Stir together. On a floured surface, knead the dough for about 5 minutes.

3. Once the dough is pliable, cover it with plastic wrap and place in a warm place for about 45 minutes, or until it almost doubles in size.

4. On a floured surface, roll out the dough until it is 10 to 12 inches in diameter.

TO MAKE THE PIZZA

1. Preheat the oven to 400°F.

2. Place the pizza dough on a ceramic pizza stone or, if you don't have one, on a baking sheet lined with parchment paper or aluminum foil. Bake for 15 minutes, until the crust is golden brown.

3. While the crust is baking, heat 1 tablespoon of oil in a non-stick skillet over medium heat. Add the onion and brown sugar. Cook until soft, about 2 minutes. Add half the sliced pears to the skillet and cook until tender, for 8 to 10 minutes. Turn off the heat and let sit.

4. Put the arugula in a large bowl. In a small bowl, whisk together the balsamic vinegar, remaining 1 tablespoon of olive oil, and salt and black pepper to taste. Drizzle it over the arugula and gently toss. Set aside.

5. Once the crust is finished baking, spread the contents from the skillet evenly on the crust. Top the pizza with the arugula. Sprinkle the other half of the sliced pears, goat cheese, and pomegranate seeds on top. Cut into 4 slices and serve.

Ingredient tip: Although it's easy to make homemade pizza dough, you can also buy it already made from the grocery store. Most grocery stores now sell whole-wheat pizza dough. If your store does not carry the whole-wheat version, you can make mini pizzas using 6- to 8-inch whole-wheat pitas.

PER SERVING (1 SLICE): Calories: 461; Total Fat: 15g; Saturated Fat: 4g; Omega-3 Fat: 144mg; Cholesterol: 7mg; Sodium: 328mg; Total Carbohydrates: 74g; Fiber: 8g; Sugars: 16g; Protein: 14g

Zucchini Lasagna

SERVES 8 TO 10 / PREP TIME: 10 MINUTES / COOK TIME: 1 HOUR 10 MINUTES

I love a good lasagna. I grew up eating it almost once a week. After getting my nutrition degree and learning that most pasta is processed and stripped of all the nutrients, I immediately began looking for alternatives. I started making lasagna with zucchini slices years before whole-wheat lasagna noodles made their debut in grocery stores. After trying the whole-wheat noodles, I still prefer the zucchini. I find this lasagna to be much lighter but just as flavorful.

4 large zucchini
1 teaspoon kosher
   salt, divided
½ tablespoon olive oil
1 white onion, diced
2 garlic cloves, minced
2 teaspoons finely chopped
   fresh thyme
1 teaspoon finely chopped
   fresh rosemary
1 tablespoon dried oregano
Freshly ground black pepper
1 (28-ounce) can diced
   tomatoes
½ cup roughly chopped
   fresh parsley,
   lightly packed
1 (8-ounce) container
   whole-milk ricotta cheese
1 large egg
Cooking spray
½ cup grated
   Parmesan cheese
4 ounces fresh mozzarella
   cheese, thinly sliced
   (about ¼ inch thick)

1. Line a large serving dish or baking sheet with paper towels.

2. Slice the zucchini into thin (⅛-inch-thick), long strips so they resemble lasagna noodles. To remove moisture, place the zucchini noodles in the serving dish and sprinkle with ½ teaspoon of salt. Layer the noodles in between paper towels. Pat softly and set aside.

3. In a large saucepan, heat the olive oil over medium heat. Add the onion and remaining ½ teaspoon of salt. Cook until translucent, 2 to 3 minutes. Add the garlic, thyme, rosemary, oregano, and black pepper to taste. Cook for another 4 to 6 minutes. Add the diced tomatoes and reduce heat to a simmer. Cover and cook for 20 minutes. After 20 minutes, turn off the heat and stir in the parsley. Adjust the seasonings to taste.

4. In a medium bowl, mix together the ricotta cheese and egg. Set aside.

5. Preheat the oven to 375°F. Coat a 9-by-12-inch glass or ceramic casserole dish with cooking spray.

6. Ladle in some sauce to coat the bottom of the prepared casserole dish. Add a layer of zucchini strips until they cover the bottom of the dish. Spread some of the ricotta cheese mixture evenly over the zucchini. Sprinkle Parmesan cheese on top of the ricotta. Repeat the layers, starting with the sauce, until the lasagna reaches about ½ inch from the top of the dish. Add the sliced mozzarella on the top.

7. Bake for 30 minutes covered, then for 10 minutes uncovered.

Variation tip: If you are looking for more veggies, try adding sautéed diced eggplant and mushrooms before the tomatoes. You can always add a few handfuls of fresh spinach 5 minutes before the sauce is done.

Always check ingredient packaging for gluten-free labeling.

PER SERVING: Calories: 188; Total Fat: 11g; Saturated Fat: 3g; Omega-3 Fat: 126mg; Cholesterol: 47mg; Sodium: 538mg; Total Carbohydrates: 13g; Fiber: 4g; Sugars: 5g; Protein: 12g

Fattoush Nachos with Hummus Drizzle

SERVES 4 / PREP TIME: 15 MINUTES / COOK TIME: 5 MINUTES

After a summer vacation to Greece, I promised myself I would make more Greek delicacies because they're so ridiculously fresh, delicious, and easy to make. Since I love salads, I figured I would switch things up and make salad "nachos" by topping toasted pita chips with a fattoush salad.

For the dressing

1 tablespoon olive oil

1 tablespoon red wine vinegar

Juice of 1 lime

1 teaspoon dried oregano

1 teaspoon ground sumac

½ teaspoon ground cumin

⅛ teaspoon kosher salt

½ teaspoon freshly ground black pepper

For the fattoush nachos

3 (6-inch) whole-wheat pitas, cut into wedges

2 cups chopped romaine lettuce

½ English cucumber, chopped

1 cup cherry tomatoes, halved

½ cup chopped fresh parsley

½ cup chopped fresh mint

¼ red onion, sliced

2 small radishes, thinly sliced

½ cup hummus

TO MAKE THE DRESSING

Whisk the olive oil, red wine vinegar, lime juice, oregano, sumac, cumin, salt, and pepper in a small bowl and set aside.

TO MAKE THE FATTOUSH NACHOS

1. Preheat the oven to 400°F.

2. Spread the pita wedges on a baking sheet. Bake for 2 to 3 minutes. Flip and bake another 3 minutes, until golden brown and crispy.

3. In a large bowl, put the romaine lettuce, English cucumber, cherry tomatoes, parsley, mint, red onion, and radish slices. Add the dressing to the bowl. Using clean hands or salad tongs, toss until combined.

4. Place the baked pita chips on a large serving tray or plate. Using tongs, transfer the salad onto the pita chips. Drizzle the hummus on top of the salad and enjoy immediately.

Substitution tip: Save time by using store-bought pita chips—just be mindful of the serving size and use 4 servings of the pita chips to make the nachos.

PER SERVING: Calories: 244; Total Fat: 8g; Saturated Fat: 1g; Omega-3 Fat: 52mg; Cholesterol: 0mg; Sodium: 361mg; Total Carbohydrates: 38g; Fiber: 8g; Sugars: 3g; Protein: 9g

Baked Eggs, Tomato, and White Bean Ragu with Cilantro Pesto

SERVES 4 / PREP TIME: 10 MINUTES / COOK TIME: 15 MINUTES

Here's another one-pot, deliciously seasoned vegetarian meal! The first time I made this dish it was actually a mistake on my part. I was hoping to make a traditional *shakshuka* but also wanted to use up leftovers that I had in my refrigerator. They were an open can of white beans, feta cheese, and leftover pesto. I decided to add it all together because, why not? It was delicious, and now it's a weeknight staple.

1 tablespoon olive oil
1 small yellow onion, diced
Kosher salt
1 (14-ounce) can crushed
  tomatoes
1 tablespoon Italian
  seasoning
1 tablespoon adobo sauce
½ teaspoon red pepper flakes
Freshly ground black pepper
1 (15.5-ounce) can white
  beans, drained and rinsed
4 eggs
1 garlic clove
½ cup fresh cilantro
⅓ cup olive oil
⅓ cup pine nuts
⅓ cup whole-wheat panko
  bread crumbs
⅓ cup crumbled feta cheese

1. In a large skillet, heat the olive oil over medium-high heat. Add the onion and season with salt. Cook for 2 to 3 minutes. Add the crushed tomatoes, Italian seasoning, adobo sauce, and red pepper flakes. Season with black pepper and stir to combine. Let simmer for 4 to 5 minutes, until the sauce has thickened.

2. Add the white beans and stir to combine. Bring to a simmer. Once simmering, crack the eggs into the skillet. Cover and simmer for 5 to 6 minutes, or until the egg whites have set.

3. Meanwhile, add the garlic, cilantro, olive oil, and pine nuts to a food processor or blender. Blend until smooth to make a pesto.

4. Drizzle the pesto over the skillet. Sprinkle with the bread crumbs and feta cheese, and serve.

Ingredient tip: I use cilantro a lot in my cooking. Some people just can't stand cilantro and describe it as having a soapy taste. Believe it or not, like or dislike for cilantro is determined by genetics. If you dislike cilantro, replacing the cilantro with basil will suffice.

PER SERVING: Calories: 547; Total Fat: 37g; Saturated Fat: 7g; Omega-3 Fat: 398mg; Cholesterol: 177mg; Sodium: 440mg; Total Carbohydrates: 38g; Fiber: 13g; Sugars: 8g; Protein: 19g

Baked Falafel with Simple Greek Yogurt Dill Sauce

SERVES 4 / PREP TIME: 15 MINUTES / COOK TIME: 30 MINUTES

I love falafel, but when I get it at restaurants, it's usually fried. I try to avoid fried foods unless it's totally worth it. For that reason, I decided to make baked falafel at home. It's just as delicious and satisfying.

For the falafel

1 (15-ounce) can chickpeas, rinsed and drained

½ yellow onion

½ cup fresh parsley

½ cup fresh cilantro

2 tablespoons tahini

3 tablespoons olive oil, divided

2 garlic cloves

½ teaspoon ground cumin

½ teaspoon kosher salt, plus more if needed

Juice of 1 lemon

Freshly ground black pepper

4 cups chopped romaine lettuce (optional)

4 whole-wheat pitas (optional)

For the sauce

½ cup 2% plain Greek yogurt

¼ small cucumber, diced

1 tablespoon chopped fresh dill

Juice of 1 lime

1 garlic clove, minced

Kosher salt

Freshly ground black pepper

TO MAKE THE FALAFEL

1. Preheat the oven to 375°F. Line a large baking sheet with parchment paper.

2. Put the chickpeas, onion, parsley, cilantro, tahini, 2 tablespoons of olive oil, garlic, cumin, salt, lemon juice, and black pepper to taste in a food processor. Pulse 15 to 20 times, until the chickpeas are chopped and the ingredients are mixed. Transfer to a large mixing bowl. Taste and adjust salt as needed.

3. Using your hands, form into 1½-inch balls. Place the falafel balls, about 1 inch apart, on the prepared baking sheet. Gently pat each ball to form a patty about ¾ inch thick.

4. Brush each falafel with the remaining 1 tablespoon of olive oil. Bake for 25 to 30 minutes, flipping the falafel once halfway through.

TO MAKE THE YOGURT DILL SAUCE

1. While the falafel is baking, add the yogurt, cucumber, dill, lime juice, and garlic to a medium bowl. Season with salt and pepper. Stir to combine

2. Serve warm falafel over a bed of lettuce or in a pita, if desired. Drizzle with a few tablespoons of sauce and enjoy.

Substitution tip: The sauce is easy, but feel free to buy pre-made tzatziki sauce from your local grocery store. It's usually found next to the hummus.

Always check ingredient packaging for gluten-free labeling.

PER SERVING: Calories: 296; Total Fat: 17g; Saturated Fat: 3g; Omega-3 Fat: 147mg; Cholesterol: 3mg; Sodium: 328mg; Total Carbohydrates: 27g; Fiber: 7g; Sugars: 6g; Protein: 12g

Lentil and Quinoa Tacos

SERVES 4 / PREP TIME: 15 MINUTES / COOK TIME: 20 MINUTES

We take Taco Tuesday very seriously in my house. We love making fish tacos, but we also love having this vegetarian taco recipe handy for when we need something filling, quick, and easy.

1 cup reduced-sodium vegetable stock

½ cup quinoa, rinsed

1 tablespoon olive oil, plus more to toast the tortillas

1 small red onion, diced

½ teaspoon kosher salt

½ cup store-bought salsa

1 teaspoon ground cumin

½ teaspoon chili powder

½ teaspoon garlic powder

Freshly ground black pepper

1 (15-ounce) can lentils, drained and rinsed

1 cup fresh or frozen corn kernels, thawed if frozen

12 corn tortillas

Juice of 1 lime

½ cup chopped fresh cilantro, lightly packed, plus more for garnish

Plain Greek yogurt, for garnish (optional)

½ cup shredded cheddar cheese (optional)

1 avocado, pitted, peeled, and diced (optional)

Lime wedges, for garnish

1. In a medium saucepan, bring the vegetable stock and quinoa to a boil. Once boiling, cover and reduce to a simmer. Simmer for 15 minutes, until the quinoa opens and fluffs up.

2. While the quinoa is cooking, in a medium pan or skillet over medium heat, heat 1 tablespoon of olive oil. Add the red onion and salt. Cook for 2 to 3 minutes. Add the salsa, cumin, chili powder, garlic powder, and black pepper to taste. Stir to combine. Add the lentils and corn and allow to slightly bubble. Remove from heat and carefully transfer contents to a large serving bowl.

3. Wipe the skillet, add a small amount of olive oil, and heat over medium to high heat. Toast the corn tortillas by heating them individually for 15 to 30 seconds on each side until darkened spots form, adding a few drizzles of olive oil as needed. Transfer each tortilla to a large serving tray once it is toasted.

4. Once the quinoa is finished cooking, add it to the bowl with the lentils. Add the lime juice and cilantro. Toss to combine.

5. Fill each tortilla with a few spoonfuls of the quinoa-lentil mixture. Top with a dollop of Greek yogurt, a sprinkle of cheese, and a few pieces of avocado, if you desire. Garnish with cilantro and a lime wedge.

Leftovers: When I make the filling for these tacos, I end up using the leftovers in many different ways throughout the week. I'll add the quinoa-lentil mixture to a bed of leafy greens to make a taco salad, use it to make a burrito, top a baked sweet potato, or stuff it inside a bell pepper. This versatile dish is easily transformed to make multiple dinners.

Always check ingredient packaging for gluten-free labeling.

PER SERVING (3 TACOS): Calories: 466; Total Fat: 12g; Saturated Fat: 2g; Omega-3 Fat: 174mg; Cholesterol: 0mg; Sodium: 612mg; Total Carbohydrates: 78g; Fiber: 15g; Sugars: 6g; Protein: 18g

7

Seafood Mains

Zucchini Noodle and Shrimp Stir-Fry, page 102

Pan-Seared Scallops Over Puréed Leeks

SERVES 4 / PREP TIME: 10 MINUTES / COOK TIME: 25 MINUTES

Not many people make scallops at home because, let's be honest, they're a bit intimidating. I used to only order scallops out until I decided to just bite the bullet and make them myself. They were surprisingly easy to make, and they cook in just a few minutes.

16 dry sea scallops

3 tablespoons olive oil, divided

2½ pounds leeks, white parts only, well washed and chopped

1 small shallot, thinly sliced

2 garlic cloves, smashed, divided

¼ cup reduced-sodium vegetable stock, plus more if needed

Kosher salt

Freshly ground black pepper

1 tablespoon butter

1 thyme sprig

1. Line a rimmed baking sheet with a clean dish towel or paper towel.

2. Place the scallops on the baking sheet and, using a second dish towel or paper towel, gently pat the scallops dry. Set aside for 10 minutes, allowing the towels to absorb the moisture from the scallops.

3. While the scallops are drying, heat 1 tablespoon of olive oil in a medium sauté pan over medium heat. Once hot, add the leeks, shallot, and 1 garlic clove. Cook for 5 minutes, or until fragrant. Add the vegetable stock. Bring to a simmer and cook, covered, for another 20 minutes, until the leeks are soft. Drain and carefully transfer the vegetables to a blender. Season with salt and pepper and blend on high until fully puréed. Transfer the purée to a bowl, cover, and set aside.

4. Wipe the sauté pan clean and heat the remaining 2 tablespoons of olive oil in the pan over high heat. Season both sides of the scallops with salt and black pepper. Once the oil is hot, add the scallops, making sure they are not touching one another. Sear for 1½ to 2 minutes.

5. Add the remaining garlic clove, butter, and thyme sprig to the pan. Using tongs, flip the scallops. Using a spoon, baste the scallops while they cook on the other side for another 1 to 1½ minutes, or until firm and centers are opaque. Transfer the scallops to a plate and cover with aluminum foil to keep warm.

6. To serve, divide the leek purée among 4 plates. Place 4 scallops on each plate and spoon any pan drippings on top. Serve warm.

Ingredient tip: When shopping for scallops, ask for dry versus wet scallops. Wet scallops are treated with a chemical solution that makes them absorb more water and appear whiter. Dry scallops do not have this additive and will have a more of a beige color.

Always check ingredient packaging for gluten-free labeling.

PER SERVING: Calories: 389; Total Fat: 15g; Saturated Fat: 4g; Omega-3 Fat: 217mg; Cholesterol: 47mg; Sodium: 339mg; Total Carbohydrates: 42g; Fiber: 4g; Sugars: 11g; Protein: 24g

Panko-Crusted Seasoned Cod with Crunchy Asparagus

SERVES 4 / PREP TIME: 5 MINUTES / COOK TIME: 15 MINUTES

It's probably the easiest dinner you can make. You can't go wrong with cod, a milder whitefish, and Old Bay, one of my favorite fish seasonings. The fish and asparagus both bake in one pan and dinner is done in 15 minutes—that's what I call a major win.

2 teaspoons Old Bay Seasoning
½ cup whole-wheat panko bread crumbs
1 pound asparagus, trimmed
1½ tablespoons olive oil, divided
4 (5-ounce) cod fillets
Juice of 1 lemon

1. Preheat the oven to 375°F. Line a rimmed baking sheet with aluminum foil or parchment paper.

2. Mix the Old Bay Seasoning and bread crumbs in a bowl and set aside.

3. Spread the asparagus on the prepared baking sheet. Drizzle 1 tablespoon of olive oil over the asparagus. Using your hands or tongs, gently toss the asparagus until evenly coated with oil. Sprinkle half of the bread crumb mixture over the asparagus, reserving the rest for the fish.

4. Pat the cod fillets dry and brush them lightly with the remaining ½ tablespoon of olive oil. Drizzle the lemon juice over the fillets.

5. Dip each fillet in the seasoned bread crumbs and then place on the same baking sheet as the asparagus.

6. Bake until the fish is no longer translucent (cut it to test) and flakes easily, 10 to 15 minutes. Serve the cod with the asparagus immediately.

Ingredient tip: Using whole-wheat panko bread crumbs really boosts the fiber. Whole-wheat bread crumbs have 4 to 5 grams of fiber in ½ cup versus 1 to 2 grams in regular bread crumbs.

PER SERVING: Calories: 236; Total Fat: 8g; Saturated Fat: 1g; Omega-3 Fat: 311mg; Cholesterol: 69mg; Sodium: 511mg; Total Carbohydrates: 14g; Fiber: 3g; Sugars: 3g; Protein: 29g

Miso-Glazed Salmon Over Sautéed Garlic Bok Choy

SERVES 4 / PREP TIME: 5 MINUTES, PLUS 1 HOUR TO MARINATE / COOK TIME: 25 MINUTES

This is my secret weapon to convert non–fish eaters into fish lovers. This marinade is the perfect combination of sweet and savory.

3 tablespoons miso paste
3 tablespoons mirin
1 tablespoon rice vinegar
1 tablespoon
　reduced-sodium soy sauce
1 tablespoon minced
　fresh ginger
Freshly ground black pepper
4 (5-ounce) salmon fillets
2 tablespoons sesame
　oil, divided
1 garlic clove, minced
1 shallot, sliced
1 bunch bok choy, chopped
2 scallions, finely chopped
Sesame seeds, for garnish

1. Whisk together the miso paste, mirin, rice vinegar, soy sauce, ginger, and black pepper to taste in a small bowl.

2. Pat the salmon fillets dry and place them in a baking dish. Pour the marinade over the salmon, and turn over each fillet until fully coated. Refrigerate for 30 to 45 minutes. Once the fish is done marinating, take it out of the refrigerator and leave it out for another 10 to 15 minutes while you cook the bok choy.

3. In a large sauté pan, heat 1 tablespoon of sesame oil over medium heat. Add the garlic and shallot, and season with salt and black pepper. Cook for 1 to 2 minutes. Add the bok choy and cook until tender, about 7 to 8 minutes. Transfer the bok choy to a dish, cover, and set aside.

4. Wipe down the pan, then add the remaining 1 tablespoon of sesame oil. Once the oil is heated, place the salmon fillets on the pan. Be sure not to crowd the fillets; you may have to cook 2 fillets at a time. Cook for 7 to 8 minutes. Flip the fillets and cook for another 2 to 3 minutes. Remove them from the pan and let them rest for 3 to 4 minutes.

5. To serve, divide the bok choy among 4 plates and place a salmon fillet on top of each. Garnish with scallions and sesame seeds.

Ingredient tip: If you want to use salmon with the skin still on, cook it skin-side down first. For thicker fillets, cook for 7 to 8 minutes; for thinner fillets, 6 to 7 minutes. Once flipped, cook thicker fillets for 2 to 3 more minutes and thinner fillets for 1 to 2 more minutes.

PER SERVING: Calories: 372; Total Fat: 23g; Saturated Fat: 4g; Omega-3 Fat: 2575mg; Cholesterol: 86mg; Sodium: 726mg; Total Carbohydrates: 12g; Fiber: 4g; Sugars: 4g; Protein: 30g

Pistachio-Crusted Salmon

SERVES 4 / PREP TIME: 10 MINUTES, PLUS 45 MINUTES TO MARINATE / COOK TIME: 15 MINUTES

I have this recipe perfected. I keep cooking it over and over and never get sick of it! The fragrant, nutty flavor and fantastic crunch from the pistachios make this dish simply mouthwatering.

4 (5-inch) salmon fillets
Kosher salt
Freshly ground black pepper
¼ cup Dijon mustard
1 tablespoon honey
Juice of 1 lemon
½ cup pistachios, shelled
    and finely chopped
½ cup whole-wheat panko
    bread crumbs

1. Preheat the oven to 400°F.

2. Pat the salmon fillets dry using a clean dish towel or paper towel. Place the salmon in a ceramic or glass dish. Season both sides with salt and black pepper.

3. In a small bowl, combine the Dijon mustard, honey, and lemon juice. Pour over the salmon and flip to ensure each side is fully coated. Let marinate in the refrigerator for 45 minutes to 1 hour.

4. In a medium bowl, combine the pistachios and bread crumbs. Dredge one side of each salmon fillet in the pistachio and bread crumb mixture and transfer to a baking sheet, breaded-side up. Pour any extra bread crumbs over each salmon fillet, pressing down gently so they stick to the fillets. Remove any bread crumbs that have fallen onto the baking sheet, as these will burn.

5. Bake for 13 to 15 minutes. Let rest for 3 to 4 minutes before serving.

Serving suggestion: Serve with your favorite vegetable or over a leafy green salad. If you are looking for a perfect pairing, I suggest Citrusy Endive Salad with Toasted Pistachios (page 60). I love adding a leftover Pistachio-Crusted Salmon fillet straight from the refrigerator to my salad the next day.

PER SERVING: Calories: 373; Total Fat: 20g; Saturated Fat: 4g; Omega-3 Fat: 2300mg; Cholesterol: 85mg; Sodium: 443mg; Total Carbohydrates: 17g; Fiber: 2g; Sugars: 6g; Protein: 32g

Bouillabaisse

SERVES 4 TO 6 / PREP TIME: 10 MINUTES / COOK TIME: 20 MINUTES

I first had bouillabaisse a few years ago while vacationing in southern France. At that time, I barely knew what it was, let alone how to pronounce it. I fell in love with this Provençal stew mainly because of the fresh variety of seafood and the distinct flavor combination from the fennel, orange zest, and saffron. It took me a while to build up the courage to make it at home. But once I finally gave it a try, I realized it wasn't difficult at all to make, and it fit my style of cooking perfectly because everything cooks right in one pot.

2 tablespoons olive oil

1 large yellow onion, sliced

2 garlic cloves, smashed

⅓ cup finely chopped
    fennel fronds

2 teaspoons grated
    orange zest

Kosher salt

Freshly ground black pepper

¼ teaspoon saffron threads

6 cups seafood stock
    (vegetable stock
    works also)

1 (14-ounce) can diced
    tomatoes

8 ounces cod, cut into
    1- to 2-inch chunks

8 ounces halibut, cut into
    1- to 2-inch chunks

8 ounces medium shrimp,
    peeled and deveined

10 clams, soaked in cold
    water for 10 minutes,
    drained, and scrubbed

10 mussels, scrubbed,
    beards removed

1 cup chopped fresh parsley

Your favorite crusty artisan
    bread, optional, for serving

1. In a large, heavy soup pot, heat the olive oil over medium to high heat. Add the onion, garlic, fennel and orange zest. Season with salt and black pepper and add the saffron. Cook for 2 to 3 minutes, until fragrant. Add seafood stock and the tomatoes. Bring to a boil.

2. Once boiling, reduce the heat and bring to a simmer. Add the cod and halibut. Cook for 7 to 8 minutes.

3. Next, add the shrimp, clams, and mussels. Cook for another 5 to 6 minutes, until the clam and mussel shells have opened, the shrimp turns pink, and the fish flakes easily with a fork. Discard any mussels or clams that haven't opened.

4. Turn off the heat, add the fresh parsley, and stir. Ladle the stew into bowls and serve warm with slices of crusty bread, if desired.

Variation tip: There are so many different ways to make this fish stew. What I've learned is that you just need to make it your own, the way that works best for you! I like keeping it simple, using premade seafood stock and keeping everything cooked in one pot. The key is to use a variety of the freshest seafood you can find. Some of my favorites are sea bass, cod, halibut, and flounder.

PER SERVING: Calories: 359; Total Fat: 13g; Saturated Fat: 2g; Omega-3 Fat: 1020mg; Cholesterol: 158mg; Sodium: 720mg; Total Carbohydrates: 16g; Fiber: 6g; Sugars: 5g; Protein: 53g

Shrimp Summer Rolls with Spicy Peanut Sauce

SERVES 5 / PREP TIME: 10 MINUTES, PLUS 30 MINUTES TO CHILL / COOK TIME: 5 MINUTES

This recipe is very versatile. It can be the perfect appetizer, lunch, or dinner when you are looking for something light and refreshing on your table. Rolling them up is a quick activity that the whole family will enjoy.

20 small shrimp, peeled and deveined

2 tablespoons peanut butter

1 tablespoon sesame oil

1 tablespoon minced or grated fresh ginger

1 tablespoon sriracha (adjust the amount to your spice preference)

1 tablespoon reduced-sodium soy sauce

2 teaspoons honey

Juice of 1 lime

10 rice paper wrappers

1 cup shredded carrots

1 red bell pepper, seeded and thinly sliced

5 scallions, trimmed and cut in half

1 cup shredded purple cabbage

1 cup roughly chopped fresh cilantro, lightly packed

1 avocado, pitted, peeled, and sliced

1. Bring a medium pot of water to a boil. Once boiling, add the shrimp. Cook for 1½ to 2 minutes, or until the shrimp turn pink. Drain and transfer the shrimp to a bowl. Let cool for a few minutes, cover, and place in the refrigerator for 30 minutes.

2. While the shrimp are cooling, make the dip by whisking together the peanut butter, sesame oil, ginger, sriracha, soy sauce, honey, and lime juice in a medium bowl. Add a few tablespoons of water to thin out the sauce until you've reached your desired consistency. Transfer the sauce to a serving bowl and set aside.

3. Prepare the rice paper wrappers according to the instructions on the package. Place the rice paper on a cutting board or flat surface. In the center of each wrapper, mound a small amount of carrots, red bell pepper, scallions, purple cabbage, cilantro, and avocado.

4. Remove the cooled shrimp from the refrigerator and add 2 shrimp to the top of each mound of filling. Roll each wrap tightly, like you would a burrito. Transfer to a serving plate and enjoy by dipping each delicious bite into the creamy sauce.

Ingredient tip: Rice paper wrappers are thin, dried pieces of dough made from rice flour. Once soaked in water for a few seconds, they become pliable and sticky. Make sure to follow the directions on the package so that your rice paper wraps are prepared correctly. If you love this dipping sauce, you'll enjoy the Spicy Tempeh Stir-Fry (page 70), which uses the same dip as the stir-fry dressing.

PER SERVING (2 ROLLS): Calories: 249; Total Fat: 12g; Saturated Fat: 2g; Omega-3 Fat: 182mg; Cholesterol: 90mg; Sodium: 292mg; Total Carbohydrates: 21g; Fiber: 4g; Sugars: 4g; Protein: 16g

Zucchini Linguine and White Clam Sauce

SERVES 4 / PREP TIME: 10 MINUTES / COOK TIME: 15 MINUTES

This recipe never fails to impress. Linguine with clams is one of my all-time favorite pasta dishes. I love ordering it out at restaurants when it's served with freshly made pasta. When I make it at home, I use zucchini noodles because they're lighter and keep me just as satisfied as regular linguine.

2 tablespoons olive
  oil, divided
1 tablespoon butter
3 garlic cloves, minced
1 shallot, sliced
Kosher salt
Freshly ground black pepper
24 littleneck clams, soaked
  in cold water for 10
  minutes, drained, and
  scrubbed
½ cup dry white wine
3 zucchini, spiralized or cut
  into ribbons
1 teaspoon red pepper flakes
½ cup grated Parmigiano-
  Reggiano cheese
½ cup chopped fresh
  parsley, lightly packed

1. In a large, heavy pot, heat 1 tablespoon of olive oil and the butter over medium heat. Add the garlic and shallot. Season with salt and pepper and cook for 1 to 2 minutes, until fragrant.

2. Add the clams and wine. Cover and cook until the clams open, about 10 minutes. Remove the clams with all the liquid and set aside in a large bowl.

3. Wipe down the emptied pot and add the remaining 1 tablespoon of oil. Once the oil is warm, add the zucchini ribbons. Cook for 3 to 4 minutes. Add the red pepper flakes and Parmigiano-Reggiano cheese. Stir until the cheese is melted.

4. Turn off the heat and add the clams and liquid back to the pot. Toss to combine and transfer to a large serving bowl. Sprinkle with the fresh parsley and serve immediately.

Ingredient tip: In place of fresh clams, you can use 1 (15-ounce) can chopped clams. Skip step 2 and instead of adding the whole clams in step 4, add the canned clams with their juice.

Always check ingredient packaging for gluten-free labeling.

PER SERVING: Calories: 218; Total Fat: 11g; Saturated Fat: 3g; Omega-3 Fat: 158mg; Cholesterol: 28mg; Sodium: 230mg; Total Carbohydrates: 13g; Fiber: 3g; Sugars: 5g; Protein: 15g

Thai Mussels

SERVES 4 TO 6 / PREP TIME: 10 MINUTES / COOK TIME: 15 MINUTES

This is the perfect example of how seafood is much easier to cook than most people think. Mussels are so tasty, fun to eat, and inexpensive. Make sure to use baguette slices—gluten-free, if necessary—to soak up the extra sauce at the bottom of the pot. You are not going to believe how tasty the leftover broth is.

2 teaspoons coconut oil

¼ cup Thai red curry paste

1 stalk lemongrass, cut into
   2-inch pieces

4 garlic cloves, sliced

1 tablespoon minced
   fresh ginger

1 (15-ounce) can
   unsweetened coconut milk

2 cups reduced-sodium
   vegetable stock

Juice of 2 limes

2 pounds mussels, scrubbed,
   beards removed

1 red chile, seeded and
   thinly sliced

1 lime, cut into wedges

1 cup chopped fresh cilantro,
   lightly packed

1. In a large pot, heat the coconut oil over medium to high heat. When the oil is hot, add the Thai red curry paste, lemongrass, garlic, and ginger. Cook for 1 to 2 minutes, until fragrant.

2. Add the coconut milk, vegetable stock, and lime juice. Bring to a boil.

3. Once the broth is boiling, add the mussels and red chile. Cover and cook for 6 to 7 minutes, or until the shells have opened. Discard mussels that remain closed after cooking.

4. Divide the mussels and broth evenly among 4 bowls. Garnish each bowl with lime wedges and fresh cilantro. Serve immediately.

Substitution tip: If you enjoy mussels, you can use the same broth from the New England Style Steamers (page 111) to cook your mussels, as well. The possibilities with mussels are truly endless.

Always check ingredient packaging for gluten-free labeling.

PER SERVING: Calories: 541; Total Fat: 38g; Saturated Fat: 27g; Omega-3 Fat: 606mg; Cholesterol: 64mg; Sodium: 1345mg; Total Carbohydrates: 23g; Fiber: 10g; Sugars: 5g; Protein: 30g

Salmon Cakes with Old Bay Yogurt Dipping Sauce

SERVES 4 / PREP TIME: 10 MINUTES / COOK TIME: 20 MINUTES

I used to make salmon cakes by blending a fresh salmon fillet in the blender and then forming the patties. Don't worry, this version will taste as fresh and delicious as using fresh salmon but will be much less expensive.

½ cup 2% plain Greek yogurt
Juice of 2 lemons, divided
1 tablespoon Old Bay Seasoning
2 (6-ounce) cans skinless salmon
½ cup fresh or frozen corn kernels, thawed if frozen
½ cup whole-wheat panko bread crumbs
2 scallions, chopped
2 large eggs
¼ cup roughly chopped fresh cilantro or parsley
Kosher salt
Freshly ground black pepper
2 tablespoons olive oil, divided

1. In a medium bowl, combine the yogurt, half of the lemon juice, and the Old Bay Seasoning. Cover and refrigerate while making the salmon cakes.

2. In a large bowl, add the canned salmon, corn, bread crumbs, scallions, eggs, cilantro, salt and black pepper to taste, and remaining lemon juice. Mix the contents with your hands until thoroughly combined.

3. Form the mixture into 8 small patties, about 3 inches in diameter and ¾-inch thick.

4. In a large skillet, heat 1 tablespoon of olive oil over medium to high heat. Add 4 salmon cakes to the skillet. Cook for 4 to 5 minutes. Flip and cook the other side for 4 to 5 minutes, or until browned and crisp. Transfer to a serving dish. Repeat with the rest of the salmon cakes, adding the remaining 1 tablespoon of oil as needed.

5. Serve warm with chilled Old Bay yogurt sauce.

Seafood tip: When shopping for canned salmon, I opt for wild-caught salmon and purchase from brands known for sustainable practices. Some canned salmon will be packed with bones. Using canned salmon with the bones adds calcium, which is great for our bones! Just take out any big bones and crush the little bones so they blend into the patty. With all the other ingredients mixed together, you won't even notice the tiny bones.

PER SERVING (2 PATTIES): Calories: 344; Total Fat: 20g; Saturated Fat: 4g; Omega-3 Fat: 2976mg; Cholesterol: 147mg; Sodium: 725mg; Total Carbohydrates: 16g; Fiber: 3g; Sugars: 3g; Protein: 26g

Zucchini Noodle and Shrimp Stir-Fry

SERVES 4 / PREP TIME: 10 MINUTES / COOK TIME: 10 MINUTES

You know you had a good meal when you can't stop thinking about it for days! That is what I experience with this stir-fry every time I make it. The first time I tested this recipe, my taste tester said, "Wow, I feel like I'm eating authentic Chinese food." I knew from that comment that this dish was a winner.

For the dressing

2 tablespoons low-sodium
   soy sauce
1 tablespoon rice vinegar
2 teaspoons brown sugar
Juice of 1 lime
1 tablespoon minced
   fresh ginger
2 garlic cloves, minced
Pinch red pepper flakes

For the stir-fry

2 tablespoons sesame
   oil, divided
1 pound shrimp, peeled and
   deveined
Kosher salt
Freshly ground black pepper
1 small yellow onion, diced
1 garlic clove, minced
1 small head broccoli,
   stemmed and cut
   into florets
2 cups sliced mushrooms
1 cup snow peas
1 cup grated carrots
3 zucchini, spiralized or cut
   into ribbons
2 scallions, thinly chopped
1 tablespoon sesame seeds

TO MAKE THE DRESSING

In a medium bowl, whisk together the soy sauce, rice vinegar, brown sugar, lime juice, ginger, garlic, and pepper flakes. Set aside.

TO MAKE THE STIR-FRY

1. Heat 1 tablespoon of sesame oil in a large skillet or wok over medium heat. Season the shrimp with salt and pepper. Once the oil is hot, add the shrimp in a single layer. Cook for 2 minutes, flip, and cook for another 1 to 2 minutes. Turn off the heat, transfer the shrimp to a bowl, cover, and set aside.

2. Wipe down the skillet, then heat ½ tablespoon of sesame oil in the skillet over medium heat. Once the oil is hot, add the onion and garlic. Cook for 1 to 2 minutes, until fragrant. Add the broccoli, mushrooms, snow peas, and carrots. Season with salt and black pepper. Cook for 5 to 7 minutes, until the vegetables soften. Once cooked, remove from the skillet and set aside in a large bowl.

3. In the same skillet, add the remaining ½ tablespoon of sesame oil. Add the zucchini noodles and cook for 3 to 4 minutes, tossing until evenly coated with oil.

4. Add the vegetables and shrimp back to the skillet. Pour the dressing over and toss until all contents are fully coated. Garnish with the scallions and sesame seeds. Serve.

Variation tip: You can make ribbons or noodles with all kinds of veggies. I love using broccoli stems and carrots to make them. You can also check out your grocery store's produce or frozen section to try out a variety of veggie noodles.

PER SERVING: Calories: 284; Total Fat: 10g; Saturated Fat: 1g; Omega-3 Fat: 671mg; Cholesterol: 180mg; Sodium: 493mg; Total Carbohydrates: 23g; Fiber: 7g; Sugars: 10g; Protein: 30g

Cauliflower Fried Rice

SERVES 6 / PREP TIME: 10 MINUTES / COOK TIME: 15 MINUTES

Have you jumped on the cauliflower rice train yet? If not, it's time to get cooking! Once you're on, you'll never get off! When incorporated into a good recipe, cauliflower rice tastes just like regular rice but has a small amount of carbs and tons of fiber—great for anyone watching their waistline or anyone who is just trying to not feel super stuffed after eating.

1 head cauliflower, cut into florets

2 tablespoons sesame oil

2 tablespoons reduced-sodium soy sauce

1 teaspoon garlic powder

3 teaspoons olive oil, divided

1 pound shrimp, peeled and deveined

Kosher salt

Freshly ground black pepper

2 cups frozen vegetable blend of corn, peas, and carrots

1 yellow onion, diced

1 cup diced fresh or canned pineapple, drained if canned

¼ cup diced scallions

1 tablespoon sesame seeds

1. Rice the cauliflower by pulsing the florets in a food processor. You may have to divide the cauliflower into 2 or 3 smaller batches. While being careful not to over-pulse, quickly pulse about 15 to 20 times, or until it has the appearance of rice. Transfer to a bowl and set aside.

2. In a small bowl, whisk together the sesame oil, soy sauce, and garlic powder. Set aside.

3. Heat 2 teaspoons of olive oil in a large sauté pan or wok over medium to high heat. Season the shrimp with salt and black pepper. Once the oil is hot, add the shrimp in a single layer. Cook for 2 minutes, flip, and cook for another 1 to 2 minutes. Turn off the heat, transfer the shrimp to a bowl, and set aside.

4. Wipe down the skillet or wok and heat again over medium heat. Add the remaining 1 teaspoon olive oil. Once the oil is warm, add the frozen vegetables and the onion. Cook for 5 to 7 minutes, or until the vegetables are thawed and warm.

5. Add the cauliflower rice. Stir to combine and cook for another 3 to 5 minutes. Once the cauliflower is tender, add the cooked shrimp and pineapple. Mix everything until all contents are evenly distributed.

6. Drizzle the dressing over the fried rice and stir to combine. Garnish with the scallions and sesame seeds. Serve.

Substitution tip: Save time by purchasing riced cauliflower from your grocery store. Most stores now offer riced vegetables either fresh in the produce section or frozen. You can also get adventurous and try different types of riced vegetables, like carrot or broccoli rice. Serve this dish with Miso-Glazed Salmon Over Sautéed Garlic Bok Choy (page 93) for a perfectly balanced and delicious meal.

PER SERVING: Calories: 200; Total Fat: 8g; Saturated Fat: 1g; Omega-3 Fat: 657mg; Cholesterol: 122mg; Sodium: 381mg; Total Carbohydrates: 12g; Fiber: 5g; Sugars: 8g; Protein: 21g

Baked Fish Sticks with Easy Honey Mustard

SERVES 4 / PREP TIME: 10 MINUTES / COOK TIME: 15 MINUTES

My toddler loves these crunchy fish fingers with honey mustard. When we have these for dinner we are both begging for more! And the best part is that they are baked instead of fried. Also, I can control what I put into them, which makes them healthier than the fish sticks in the frozen section of any grocery store.

For the fish sticks

1 cup whole-wheat panko bread crumbs

2 teaspoons dried oregano

1 teaspoon paprika

½ teaspoon kosher salt

2 large eggs, beaten

¾ cup all-purpose flour

1 pound cod fillets, cut into strips (1 inch wide and 3 inches long)

For the honey mustard

½ cup Dijon mustard

⅓ cup honey

Juice of ½ lemon

¼ teaspoon ground cayenne pepper

Kosher salt

Freshly ground black pepper

TO MAKE THE FISH STICKS

1. Preheat the oven to 400°F. Line a baking sheet with aluminum foil or parchment paper.

2. Mix together the bread crumbs, oregano. paprika, and salt in a shallow medium bowl. Put the egg in another shallow bowl and the flour in a third shallow bowl.

3. Dredge a strip of fish in the flour until fully coated. Shake off any excess flour. Dip the fish in the egg, followed by the bread crumb mixture. Pat the fish to ensure the coating adheres. Place the fish on the prepared baking sheet. Repeat with the rest of the fish strips.

4. Bake for 10 to 12 minutes, until the fish flakes easily with a fork, flipping once at the halfway point.

5. Serve the fish sticks when they are still warm with a healthy amount of honey mustard.

TO MAKE THE HONEY MUSTARD

In a medium bowl, mix the Dijon mustard, honey, lemon juice, cayenne pepper, and salt and black pepper to taste.

Leftovers: If you have extra honey mustard, store it in the refrigerator in an airtight container for up to 4 days. I love thinning it out with a few tablespoons of water and a tablespoon of apple cider vinegar to use as a salad dressing.

PER SERVING: Calories: 430; Total Fat: 6g; Saturated Fat: 1g; Omega-3 Fat: 239mg; Cholesterol: 133mg; Sodium: 834mg; Total Carbohydrates: 63g; Fiber: 3g; Sugars: 26g; Protein: 30g

Herbed Cod with Summer Vegetables

SERVES 4 / PREP TIME: 5 MINUTES / COOK TIME: 20 MINUTES

I'm not a trained chef, but I always feel like one when I make the elegant, fancy pan sauce with white wine for this dish. The best part about this recipe is that it's another one-pot meal that cooks fast and has minimal cleanup.

4 (6-ounce) cod fillets

Kosher salt

Freshly ground black pepper

1 teaspoon olive oil

1 large or 2 smaller zucchini, sliced or diced

2 cups fresh or frozen corn kernels, thawed if frozen

1 tablespoon vegetable oil

2 garlic cloves, smashed

3 thyme sprigs

2 small shallots, sliced

Juice of 2 lemons

1 tablespoon butter

¾ cup dry white wine

1. Using a clean dish towel or paper towel, pat the fish dry. Season both sides with salt and pepper. Set aside.

2. To make the veggie side, heat the olive oil in a large sauté pan over medium heat. Add the zucchini and corn kernels, and season with salt and black pepper. Toss for 4 to 5 minutes until fully heated. Transfer to a bowl, cover, and set aside.

3. To the same sauté pan, add 1 tablespoon of vegetable oil over medium to high heat. Once the oil is hot, add the cod fillets, garlic, thyme sprigs, shallots, and lemon juice. Cook the fillets for 5 to 6 minutes. Turn the fish over and cook for another 3 to 4 minutes, basting with the liquid. The fish should be browned on both sides and opaque. Transfer the fillets to a serving tray, leaving all the other contents in the pan. Cover the cod with aluminum foil to keep warm. ➤

4. To make the pan sauce, add the butter to the skillet and stir. Gently scrape the bottom of the pan to loosen the brown cooked bits. Add the wine and boil until the sauce thickens, 2 to 3 minutes. Adjust the seasoning with salt and black pepper. Discard the thyme sprigs.

5. To serve, divide the zucchini and corn mixture evenly among 4 plates. Top each plate with a cod fillet. Pour the pan sauce evenly over each fillet.

Variation tip: Although the veggie side is super easy, it does add a few extra minutes. If you don't have much time, go ahead and use a steam-in-the-bag package of vegetables and prepare them as you are cooking the fish. You still have a quick, easy, and delicious dinner that is equally as fancy.

Always check ingredient packaging for gluten-free labeling.

PER SERVING: Calories: 306; Total Fat: 10g; Saturated Fat: 3g; Omega-3 Fat: 284mg; Cholesterol: 68mg; Sodium: 190mg; Total Carbohydrates: 16g; Fiber: 3g; Sugars: 4g; Protein: 32g

Sole en Papillote

SERVES 4 / PREP TIME: 10 MINUTES / COOK TIME: 15 MINUTES

This simple fish *en papillote*—also known as fish in parchment—is just as easy to cook as it is to clean up! The fish is steamed in parchment paper, allowing the lemon and herbs to infuse the fish and bok choy with all of their delicious flavors.

4 (4-ounce) sole fillets
Kosher salt
Freshly ground black pepper
2 shallots, diced
1 tablespoon capers
4 heads baby bok choy
4 garlic cloves, smashed
4 thyme sprigs
1 tablespoon olive oil
1 lemon, thinly sliced

1. Preheat the oven to 400°F.

2. Pat the fish dry with a paper towel. Fold 4 pieces of parchment paper in half and open them back up. Place 1 fillet on one half of each piece of parchment paper. Season both sides of each fillet with salt and black pepper.

3. Divide the shallots and capers among the fillets. Then place 1 head bok choy, 1 smashed garlic clove, and 1 thyme sprig on top of each fillet. Brush with olive oil and top with lemon slices.

4. Fold the other side of the parchment over and crimp the edges tightly closed. Place the packages on a large rimmed baking sheet.

5. Bake for 10 to 12 minutes. Once done baking, carefully (the steam will be hot!) cut the pouches open. Serve warm.

Serving suggestion: Make sure you cut the parchment paper big enough to cover the entire fillet. It's always better to have a piece that is too big rather than too small. If you don't have parchment, aluminum foil will work as well.

PER SERVING: Calories: 143; Total Fat: 6g; Saturated Fat: 1g; Omega-3 Fat: 341mg; Cholesterol: 55mg; Sodium: 216mg; Total Carbohydrates: 3g; Fiber: 1g; Sugars: 1g; Protein: 22g

Tikka Masala Spiced Cod

SERVES 4 / PREP TIME: 5 MINUTES / COOK TIME: 15 MINUTES

When we think of tikka masala, it is usually the version that comes in the form of a creamy, buttery sauce. For this recipe, you will get a lighter, pescatarian version with all the great flavors and spice of the tikka masala you love but in a healthier way.

4 (4-inch) cod fillets
2 tablespoons tikka masala spice mix
1 tablespoon curry powder
Kosher salt
Freshly ground black pepper
1 tablespoon olive oil
1 shallot, sliced
3 garlic cloves, smashed
2 thyme sprigs
¾ cup dry white wine

1. Pat the cod fillets dry using a dish towel or paper towel. In a small bowl, mix together the tikka masala mix, curry powder, and salt and black pepper to taste. Season both sides of each fish fillet with the spice mixture.

2. In a large sauté pot, heat the olive oil over high heat. Once the oil is hot, add the cod fillets, shallot, garlic, and thyme sprigs to the pan. Cook the fillets for 5 to 6 minutes. Flip the fish over and cook for another 3 to 4 minutes, basting with the liquid. The fish should be browned on both sides and opaque. Transfer the fillets to a serving tray, leaving the other contents in the pan. Cover the cod with aluminum foil to keep warm.

3. Add the wine to the skillet. Gently scrape the bottom of the pan to loosen the brown cooked bits. Boil until the sauce thickens and reduces, 2 to 3 minutes. Remove the thyme sprigs and pour the sauce over the fish fillets. Serve warm.

Serving suggestion: If you are looking for the perfect vegetable pairing with this dish, I suggest Turmeric-Spiced Crispy Cauliflower (page 126).

Always check ingredient packaging for gluten-free labeling.

PER SERVING: Calories: 167; Total Fat: 5g; Saturated Fat: 1g; Omega-3 Fat: 221mg; Cholesterol: 40mg; Sodium: 122mg; Total Carbohydrates: 3g; Fiber: 0g; Sugars: 0g; Protein: 20g

New England Style Steamers

SERVES 4 / PREP TIME: 1 HOUR / COOK TIME: 15 MINUTES

Want to be as happy as a clam? Where does that saying come from, anyway? All I know is that I'm always super happy when eating these clams. Steamers are also known as soft-shell clams or long-neck clams. They have a long, protruding neck, known as a siphon. I love simply steaming these clams and dipping them in a sauce or adding them to a chowder.

3 pounds soft-shell or
　long-neck clams
Kosher salt
2 tablespoons butter
2 shallots, sliced
Freshly ground black pepper
3 garlic cloves, smashed
2 thyme sprigs
1 cup white wine
Juice from 1 lemon
½ cup roughly chopped
　fresh parsley,
　lightly packed

1. Rinse the clams under cold water and transfer them to a large bowl. Fill the bowl with cold water so that the water level is 2 to 3 inches above the top of the clams. Add ⅓ cup of salt to the water. Using your hands, gently stir the water so that the salt gets evenly distributed among the clams. Set aside to soak for 1 hour, then drain and rinse to remove any excess grit.

2. Add the butter to a large pot over medium heat. Once the butter is melted, add the shallots, season with salt and black pepper, and cook for 2 minutes. Add the garlic, thyme, white wine, and lemon juice. Once boiling, add the clams gently to the pot. Cover and cook for 7 to 8 minutes, or until the clams have opened.

3. Divide the clams among 4 large serving bowls. Sprinkle parsley over each bowl. Serve with slices of a multigrain baguette, if the carbs and the gluten are okay for you.

Ingredient tip: Before prepping the clams, check thoroughly for any cracks or damage to the shell, discarding any that don't make the cut. Unlike hard-shell clams, live soft-shell clams often remain slightly open because of their siphon. If a clam appears to be open, gently tap it on the counter. If it doesn't respond by retracting its siphon a bit, discard it, as well.

Always check ingredient packaging for gluten-free labeling.

PER SERVING: Calories: 150; Total Fat: 6g; Saturated Fat: 4g; Omega-3 Fat: 123mg; Cholesterol: 33mg; Sodium: 119mg; Total Carbohydrates: 5g; Fiber: 1g; Sugars: 1g; Protein: 7g

Grilled Mahi-Mahi Wrap

SERVES 4 / PREP TIME: 10 MINUTES / COOK TIME: 15 MINUTES

I love a good wrap, especially for lunch. I started making this wrap when I got tired of my usual healthy lunch ideas. You can eat only so many tuna salad wraps, right? Add this to your work lunch rotation to switch things up a bit.

1½ cups shredded cabbage mix

2 scallions, green parts only, chopped

⅓ cup chopped fresh cilantro, lightly packed

Juice of 1 lime, plus more if you desire

Kosher salt

4 (4-ounce) mahi-mahi fillets

Freshly ground black pepper

½ teaspoon ground cumin

Pinch ground cayenne pepper

2 teaspoons olive oil

4 (6- to 8-inch) whole-wheat wraps

1 avocado, pitted, peeled, and quartered

1 small tomato, sliced

½ red onion, sliced

1. Preheat the grill to medium-high heat.

2. While the grill is warming up, make the coleslaw. Add the shredded cabbage mix, scallions, cilantro, and lime juice to a bowl and season with salt. Toss and set aside.

3. Pat the fish dry with a dish towel or paper towel. In a small bowl, combine salt and black pepper to taste, cumin, and cayenne pepper. Brush both sides of each fillet with the olive oil and sprinkle both sides with the seasoning mixture. Grill for 4 to 5 minutes per side, until golden brown on the outside and opaque in the center.

4. Assemble the wraps. In the center of each wrap, add a spoonful of coleslaw, smash a quarter of the avocado, add a few tomato slices and a sprinkle of red onion, and top with a mahi-mahi fillet. Finish with another squeeze of fresh lime juice, if you like.

5. Wrap as you would a burrito, cut in half, and serve.

Variation tip: All of these ingredients make for a great taco, as well. If you're in the mood for tacos, just swap the wrap for a hard or soft taco shell. When using this recipe to make mahi-mahi tacos, I recommend garnishing with a fresh squeeze of lime juice and a sprinkle of cilantro.

PER SERVING: Calories: 340; Total Fat: 14g; Saturated Fat: 1g; Omega-3 Fat: 656mg; Cholesterol: 40mg; Sodium: 294mg; Total Carbohydrates: 28g; Fiber: 6g; Sugars: 3g; Protein: 26g

Seafood Paella with Sweet Plantains

SERVES 4 TO 6 / PREP TIME: 15 MINUTES / COOK TIME: 1 HOUR

Do you ever go to a restaurant and ask for a simple swap and in return get the "no substitutions" response? This happened to me when I was ordering a seafood paella and noticed plantains on the menu. I asked for the plantains to be mixed into the paella, but unfortunately, I guess that wasn't possible. I ended up ordering the seafood paella with a side of plantains and added them to the dish myself. I enjoyed it so much that plantains have been a staple ingredient in my paellas ever since.

1 tablespoon olive oil

1 yellow or white
  onion, sliced

Kosher salt

Freshly ground black pepper

3 garlic cloves, minced

1½ teaspoons paprika

1 teaspoon ground cumin

½ teaspoon ground
  cayenne pepper

3 or 4 strands saffron

1¾ cups reduced-sodium
  vegetable stock

4 ripe plum
  tomatoes, chopped

¾ cup brown rice

2 teaspoons coconut oil

1 very ripe plantain, peeled
  and cut into ¼-inch pieces

10 medium shrimp, peeled
  and deveined

10 mussels, scrubbed,
  beards removed

10 clams, soaked in cold
  water for 10 minutes,
  drained, and scrubbed

½ cup frozen peas, thawed

½ cup roughly chopped
  fresh parsley

1. Preheat the oven to 400°F. Line a baking sheet with aluminum foil or parchment paper.

2. In a large paella pan or cast-iron skillet, heat the olive oil over medium heat. Add the onion, season with salt and black pepper, and cook for 2 to 3 minutes. Add the garlic, paprika, cumin, cayenne pepper, and saffron and cook for 1 minute.

3. Next, add the vegetable stock, tomatoes, and rice. Bring to a simmer, cover, and cook for 30 to 35 minutes.

4. While the rice is cooking, heat the coconut oil in the microwave for 30 seconds at a time until fully melted. Add the coconut oil and plantain to a medium bowl and toss until coated. Spread the plantain pieces out on the prepared baking sheet. Bake for 10 to 12 minutes, until the plantain is golden brown.

5. Once the rice is tender and the stock is just about absorbed, add the shrimp, mussels, and clams, gently pressing each piece into the rice. Cover and cook for 8 to 10 minutes, until the clams and mussels open and the shrimp turn pink. Discard any clams or mussels that did not open.

6. Stir in the peas and plantain. Cover and cook for another 3 to 4 minutes. Remove from heat, garnish with the fresh parsley, and serve. ➤

Substitution tip: Save time by using precooked brown rice. Grocery stores now sell precooked microwavable brown rice or fully cooked, frozen brown rice. It will save you 25 to 30 minutes of cook time in this recipe, which is really great!

Always check ingredient packaging for gluten-free labeling.

PER SERVING: Calories: 409; Total Fat: 10g; Saturated Fat: 4g; Omega-3 Fat: 412mg; Cholesterol: 134mg; Sodium: 478mg; Total Carbohydrates: 56g; Fiber: 6g; Sugars: 12g; Protein: 27g

Seared Sea Bass with Caponata

SERVES 4 / PREP TIME: 10 MINUTES / COOK TIME: 40 MINUTES

This caponata sauce will pair perfectly with any whitefish. I find sea bass to be my favorite. You can always sauté the tomatoes and eggplants on the stove for the caponata, which is the more traditional method. However, after making this dish so much, I've come to really love the taste of the roasted vegetables.

1 medium eggplant, cut into
½-inch cubes
1 pint cherry tomatoes
3 tablespoons olive
oil, divided
Kosher salt
Freshly ground black pepper
1 red onion, diced
3 garlic cloves, minced
¼ cup black olives, pitted
and chopped
3 tablespoons
red wine vinegar or
balsamic vinegar
1 tablespoon dried capers
⅓ cup chopped fresh basil,
lightly packed
⅓ cup chopped fresh parsley,
lightly packed
4 (4-ounce) sea bass fillets
¼ cup pine nuts

1. Preheat the oven to 400°F. Line a baking sheet with aluminum foil or parchment paper.

2. In a large mixing bowl, place the eggplant and tomatoes. Drizzle them with 1 tablespoon of oil and season with salt and black pepper. Toss to combine. Transfer to the prepared baking sheet and bake for 15 to 20 minutes.

3. In a large sauté pan, heat 1 tablespoon of oil over medium heat. Once hot, add the red onion. Season with salt and pepper and cook for 1 to 2 minutes. Add the garlic and cook for another minute. Then, add the olives, vinegar, and capers and cook for 3 to 4 minutes.

4. Once the eggplant and tomatoes are finished roasting, add them to the skillet. Stir to combine. Cook until the sauce thickens, 4 to 5 minutes. Turn off the heat and add the basil and parsley. Stir to combine. Cover to keep warm while cooking the fish. ➤

5. Pat the fish dry and season both sides with salt and pepper. In another large sauté pan, heat the remaining 1 tablespoon of oil over medium-high heat. Once the oil is hot, place the sea bass in the pan. Cook for 3 to 4 minutes. Flip and cook for another 3 minutes.

6. To serve, place a piece of fish on each plate. Place a scoop of caponata and a sprinkle of pine nuts over the fish.

Serving suggestion: I enjoy pairing this dish with whole-wheat or multigrain pasta. But it also goes really well with your favorite veggie noodle, if you want to keep it low-carb and gluten-free.

Always check ingredient packaging for gluten-free labeling.

PER SERVING: Calories: 404; Total Fat: 30g; Saturated Fat: 5g; Omega-3 Fat: 863mg; Cholesterol: 43mg; Sodium: 305mg; Total Carbohydrates: 17g; Fiber: 6g; Sugars: 8g; Protein: 22g

Shrimp and Pesto Grilled Pizza

SERVES 6 TO 8 / PREP TIME: 20 MINUTES / COOK TIME: 25 MINUTES

Who would have thought grilling pizza would be so fun? During the summer, my daughter and I set up a pizza-topping station outside on our deck. We grill individual pizzas and create our own masterpieces. I love switching up pizza toppings to offer some variety outside of the traditional red sauce and cheese. If you also like exploring new toppings, you will love this pesto-and-shrimp-topped pizza.

For the pesto

1 garlic clove
½ cup fresh basil, plus a few leaves for garnish
⅓ cup olive oil
⅓ cup pine nuts
¼ cup grated Parmigiano-Reggiano cheese, plus ¼ cup to sprinkle at the end
Kosher salt
Freshly ground black pepper

For the sauce

1 tablespoon olive oil, plus 1 teaspoon if needed
1 garlic clove, minced
1 small yellow onion, diced
Kosher salt
Freshly ground black pepper
1 pint cherry tomatoes, halved
2 cups white mushrooms, sliced

TO MAKE THE PESTO

Put the garlic, basil, olive oil, pine nuts, ¼ cup Parmigiano-Reggiano cheese, and salt and black pepper to taste in a food processor or blender. Blend until smooth. Set aside.

TO MAKE THE SAUCE

In a medium sauté pan, heat 1 tablespoon of olive oil over medium heat. Add the garlic and onion. Season with salt and black pepper and cook for 1 to 2 minutes, until fragrant. Add the cherry tomatoes and mushrooms, and cook for another 7 to 8 minutes, adding 1 teaspoon of oil if the pan gets dry. While cooking, smash the tomatoes lightly. Transfer to a bowl and set aside.

TO MAKE THE PIZZAS

1. Preheat the grill to high heat. Make sure the grill grates are clean, then oil them with vegetable oil.

2. While the grill is heating up, prepare the pizza dough. On a floured surface, roll out the dough to form either 1 larger pizza or 2 smaller pizzas a little less than ½-inch thick. Brush one side of the dough with ½ tablespoon of olive oil.

3. Once the grill is hot, grill the shrimp over high heat for 1 to 2 minutes on each side. Set aside on a plate. ➤

For the pizzas

Vegetable oil, for oiling grill grates

1 store-bought whole-wheat pizza dough or honey wheat pizza dough (see page 78)

All-purpose flour, for dusting work surface

1 tablespoon olive oil, divided

10 to 14 shrimp, peeled and deveined

4. Before transferring the pizza dough to the grill, make sure you have the sautéed tomato and mushroom mixture, shrimp, and pesto nearby. You will be assembling the pizza over the grill.

5. Place the oiled side of the pizza dough facedown on the grill grates. Brush the top side of the dough with the remaining ½ tablespoon of olive oil. Cook for 3 to 4 minutes, until the dough becomes slightly crispy and golden brown. Flip and cook for another 1 to 2 minutes. Turn off the grill.

6. Assemble your pizza by evenly spreading the tomato and mushroom mixture as your sauce, followed by the grilled shrimp. Drizzle the pesto over the pizza. Garnish with the remaining ¼ cup of Parmigiano-Reggiano and remaining basil leaves. Remove from the grill carefully. Cut into 6 to 8 slices and enjoy!

Ingredient tip: If you make your own dough, double the recipe and freeze whatever you do not use. Simply coat it with oil, put it in a freezer bag, and squeeze out the excess air. Freeze for up to 4 months. When ready to make pizza again, defrost in the refrigerator the day before use.

PER SERVING: Calories: 456; Total Fat: 25g; Saturated Fat: 4g; Omega-3 Fat: 427mg; Cholesterol: 84mg; Sodium: 377mg; Total Carbohydrates: 41g; Fiber: 4g; Sugars: 6g; Protein: 19g

Halibut with Shaved Fennel and Citrus Salad

SERVES 4 / PREP TIME: 10 MINUTES / COOK TIME: 15 MINUTES

I love making salads with fennel because the bulb of the fennel plant has a very mild licorice taste that even non–licorice lovers will enjoy. Fennel also offers a crisp texture that is perfect when eaten raw or sautéed.

2 tablespoons olive
  oil, divided
3 tablespoons sherry vinegar
2 teaspoons honey
Juice of 1 lemon
2 tablespoons grated
  orange zest
2 bulbs fennel, cored and
  thinly shaved
¼ cup fresh mint, plus
  2 tablespoons
Kosher salt
Freshly ground black pepper
2 oranges, peeled and sliced
¼ cup pistachios,
  roughly chopped
4 (4-ounce) halibut fillets
1 clove garlic, sliced
1 shallot, sliced
2 thyme leaves and sprigs
1 tablespoon butter

1. To make the dressing, whisk together 1 tablespoon of olive oil, the sherry vinegar, honey, lemon juice, and orange zest.

2. Put the shaved fennel and ¼ cup of mint in a large bowl and drizzle with the dressing. Season with salt and black pepper. Add the orange slices and toss. Sprinkle the salad with the pistachios. Set aside.

3. Pat the fish dry and season both sides with salt and black pepper. In a large skillet, heat 1 tablespoon of olive oil over medium-high heat. Add the garlic and shallot. Cook for 1 to 2 minutes, until fragrant. Add the thyme and halibut fillets. Cook for 3 to 4 minutes, then add the butter. Once the butter is melted, flip the fillets and baste with the butter. Cook the other side for another 4 to 5 minutes, until the fish is opaque and flakes with a fork.

4. To serve, transfer the fennel salad to a serving dish and place the halibut on top. Garnish with the remaining 2 tablespoons of mint and enjoy.

Seafood tip: Halibut is a mild whitefish and has a similar taste, texture, and appearance to cod. I use the two types of fish in recipes interchangeably, which allows me to buy whichever one is on sale at my grocery store.

Always check ingredient packaging for gluten-free labeling.

PER SERVING: Calories: 331; Total Fat: 14g; Saturated Fat: 4g; Omega-3 Fat: 674mg; Cholesterol: 68mg; Sodium: 253mg; Total Carbohydrates: 26g; Fiber: 7g; Sugars: 12g; Protein: 29g

Lemony Flounder with Creamy Cashew Alfredo Zucchini Noodles

SERVES 4 / PREP TIME: 5 MINUTES, PLUS 30 MINUTES TO SOAK / COOK TIME: 10 MINUTES

The cashew Alfredo in this recipe is creamy and cheesy, despite not having any cream or cheese at all! The blended cashews add to the creamy texture, while the nutritional yeast offers the cheesy taste. This is a great dairy-free alternative to traditional Alfredo sauce. Serve with zucchini noodles for a complete, delicious meal.

For the cashew Alfredo sauce

½ cup cashews

1 cup unsweetened plain almond milk

2 tablespoons nutritional yeast

½ teaspoon paprika

¼ teaspoons kosher salt

Juice of 1 lemon

For the flounder and zucchini ribbons

4 (5-ounce) flounder fillets

Juice of 1 lemon

Kosher salt

Freshly ground black pepper

1 tablespoon olive oil

1 shallot, sliced

1 clove garlic, sliced

3 large zucchinis, spiralized or cut into ribbons

1 cup frozen peas

¼ cup finely chopped fresh parsley leaves

TO MAKE THE SAUCE

1. Soak the cashews in hot water for 30 minutes. Drain.

2. Add the softened cashews, almond milk, nutritional yeast, paprika, salt, and lemon juice to a blender or food processor. Blend until smooth. Set aside.

TO MAKE THE FLOUNDER AND NOODLES

1. Preheat the oven to 400°F. Line a baking sheet with aluminum foil or parchment paper.

2. Coat both sides of the flounder with lemon juice and season both sides with salt and black pepper. Transfer to the prepared baking sheet and bake for 10 to 12 minutes, until the fish is opaque and flakes with a fork.

3. Meanwhile, in a large sauté pan, heat the olive oil over medium heat. Add the shallot, season with salt and pepper, and cook for 1 to 2 minutes. Add the garlic and cook for another 1 to 2 minutes. Stir the cashew Alfredo sauce into the pan.

4. Once the sauce is bubbling, add the zucchini and frozen peas. Cook and toss until everything is heated.

5. To serve, evenly divide the zucchini ribbons among 4 plates. Place a flounder fillet over each serving of zucchini ribbons. Garnish with the fresh parsley.

Variation tip: This creamy Alfredo sauce would also go great over veggie noodles with clams and mussels. If you have leftover sauce, store it in the refrigerator for up to 3 days or freeze for up to 4 months in an airtight container or ice cube tray. Once ready to use, thaw in the refrigerator the night before, or add to a pot while frozen and reheat on the stove over low heat.

Always check ingredient packaging for gluten-free labeling.

PER SERVING: Calories: 372; Total Fat: 15g; Saturated Fat: 2g; Omega-3 Fat: 457mg; Cholesterol: 69mg; Sodium: 372mg; Total Carbohydrates: 26g; Fiber: 8g; Sugars: 7g; Protein: 38g

Snacks and Sides

Turmeric-Spiced Crispy Cauliflower, page 126

Quinoa Salsa with Mango and Black Beans

SERVES 6 TO 8 / PREP TIME: 10 MINUTES / COOK TIME: 15 MINUTES

I love making this quinoa salsa and leaving it in the refrigerator to incorporate into meals during the workweek. I'll use it as a side dish at dinner, scoop it on top of a salad for lunch, or devour it with tortilla chips as a snack. Whichever way you decide to eat it, I know you'll enjoy this salad as much as I do.

1 cup quinoa, rinsed

Juice of 2 limes

2 tablespoons olive oil

Kosher salt

Freshly ground black pepper

1 (15-ounce) can no-salt-
added black beans,
drained and rinsed

1 cup fresh or frozen corn
kernels, thawed if frozen

1 ripe mango, peeled
and diced

½ red onion, finely chopped

½ cup roughly chopped
fresh cilantro,
lightly packed

1 jalapeño pepper,
seeded, deveined, and
finely chopped

1. Cook the quinoa according to the package instructions and set aside in a large serving bowl.

2. In a small bowl, whisk together the lime juice, olive oil, and salt and black pepper to taste. Set aside.

3. To the large bowl with the quinoa, add the black beans, corn kernels, mango, red onion, cilantro, and jalapeño pepper. Toss and add the dressing. Mix until everything is fully coated. Taste and adjust the seasoning as needed. Serve warm or chilled, and enjoy as is or over a bed of greens.

Substitution tip: When I'm in a hurry and don't have much time, I replace the mango, onion, cilantro, jalapeño pepper, and lime juice with a container of premade fresh mango salsa from my local grocery store. To save even more time, I'll use a packet of precooked quinoa and simply add corn and black beans.

PER SERVING: Calories: 245; Total Fat: 7g; Saturated Fat: 1g; Omega-3 Fat: 182mg; Cholesterol: 0mg; Sodium: 34mg; Total Carbohydrates: 40g; Fiber: 6g; Sugars: 10g; Protein: 8g

Baked Ricotta with Basil-Pistachio Pesto

SERVES 8 TO 10 / PREP TIME: 5 MINUTES / COOK TIME: 30 MINUTES

Envision a thick, toasted slice of multigrain bread dipped in warm, gooey baked ricotta, dripping in delicious basil-pistachio pesto. You're not dreaming. You, too, can have this decadent ricotta dish in the comfort of your own home. Don't wait another second—get in the kitchen and start making this dish right now!

1 pint cherry
  tomatoes, halved
6 tablespoons olive
  oil, divided
1 (8-ounce) container
  whole-milk ricotta cheese
1 large egg
Kosher salt
Freshly ground black pepper
1 cup fresh basil,
  lightly packed
1 garlic clove
⅓ cup pistachios, shelled
⅓ cup grated Pecorino
  Romano cheese
Multigrain loaf, sliced
  and toasted

1. Preheat the oven to 375°F.

2. Place the tomatoes in a medium bowl and drizzle with 2 tablespoons of olive oil. Toss until coated. Set aside.

3. In another medium bowl, mix together the ricotta cheese and egg, and season with salt and black pepper. Transfer the ricotta mixture to a medium cast-iron skillet. Set aside.

4. To make the pesto, put the basil, garlic, pistachios, and Pecorino Romano cheese in a blender or food processor. Pulse while adding the remaining 4 tablespoons of olive oil slowly as the contents become blended.

5. Pour the pesto over the ricotta and spread evenly. Arrange the tomatoes on top and bake for 30 to 40 minutes.

6. Serve warm with toasted bread.

Leftovers: I love making pesto and when I do, I double or even triple the recipe so that I have extra for when I need it. If you do the same, simply freeze it in a plastic container or in an ice cube tray. Just defrost in the refrigerator for 1 to 2 days before use, or heat while frozen on the stove top over low heat.

PER SERVING: Calories: 275; Total Fat: 16g; Saturated Fat: 5g; Omega-3 Fat: 143mg; Cholesterol: 38mg; Sodium: 356mg; Total Carbohydrates: 22g; Fiber: 5g; Sugars: 5g; Protein: 11g

Turmeric-Spiced Crispy Cauliflower

SERVES 4 / PREP TIME: 5 MINUTES / COOK TIME: 30 MINUTES

Cauliflower is one of the most versatile vegetables out there! When I want to keep it simple, I love roasted cauliflower florets with a variety of spices, especially turmeric, which adds a beautiful golden glow and powerful anti-inflammatory properties.

1 head cauliflower, cut
   into florets
1 tablespoon olive oil
2 teaspoons ground
   turmeric
1 teaspoon ground cumin
½ teaspoon ground
   cayenne pepper
Kosher salt
Freshly ground black pepper

1. Preheat the oven to 400°F. Line a rimmed baking sheet with aluminum foil or parchment paper.

2. In a large mixing bowl, combine the cauliflower florets, olive oil, turmeric, cumin, cayenne pepper, and salt and black pepper to taste. Toss until evenly coated, and transfer to the prepared baking sheet.

3. Bake for 25 to 30 minutes, until the cauliflower is browned and slightly crispy.

Variation tip: Make a cauliflower soup by following this recipe, then puréeing the roasted florets in the blender with 4 cups vegetable stock. You can serve it hot or cold.

PER SERVING: Calories: 89; Total Fat: 4g; Saturated Fat: 1g; Omega-3 Fat: 103mg; Cholesterol: 0mg; Sodium: 103mg; Total Carbohydrates: 12g; Fiber: 6g; Sugars: 5g; Protein: 4g

Cucumber Shrimp Bites with Spicy Mayo

SERVES 6 TO 8 / PREP TIME: 10 MINUTES, PLUS 30 MINUTES
TO MARINATE / COOK TIME: 10 MINUTES

These cucumber shrimp bites are the perfect appetizer for a dinner party or holiday party. They're super easy to make and so flavorful. They remind me of sushi but without the rice.

1 tablespoon sesame
  oil, divided
2 teaspoons
  reduced-sodium soy sauce
1 teaspoon grated
  fresh ginger
Juice of 1 lime
16 small shrimp, peeled and
  deveined
1 tablespoon sriracha
¼ cup mayonnaise
1 large English cucumber,
  peeled and cut into
  ¼-inch-thick rounds
2 tablespoons chopped
  scallions
1 tablespoon sesame seeds

1. In a large bowl, whisk together ½ tablespoon of sesame oil, soy sauce, ginger, and lime juice. Add the shrimp to the bowl and toss until fully coated. Cover and refrigerate for 30 to 45 minutes.

2. Make the spicy mayo by mixing together the sriracha and mayonnaise in a small bowl. Set aside.

3. In a nonstick sauté pan or cast-iron skillet over medium heat, heat the remaining ½ tablespoon of sesame oil. Add the shrimp to the pan in a single layer. Cook for 2 minutes, flip, and cook for another 1 to 2 minutes. Transfer to a bowl and set aside.

4. Arrange the cucumber rounds on a serving tray. Using a small spoon, add a dollop of spicy mayo to each cucumber. Top each cucumber slice with a shrimp. Garnish with the scallions and sesame seeds. Serve warm or chilled (place in the refrigerator for 30 minutes before serving).

Substitution tip: If you're looking for a healthy swap, replace the mayo with 2% plain Greek yogurt. It tastes almost identical and offers more protein and fewer calories.

PER SERVING: Calories: 161; Total Fat: 8g; Saturated Fat: 1g; Omega-3 Fat: 78mg; Cholesterol: 116mg; Sodium: 261mg; Total Carbohydrates: 6g; Fiber: 2g; Sugars: 1g; Protein: 16g

Salmon and Roasted Eggplant Dip

SERVES 6 TO 8 / PREP TIME: 5 MINUTES / COOK TIME: 45 MINUTES

I love good, smoky baba ghanoush, a delicious eggplant dip. The smoked salmon makes this twist on the traditional dip even smokier and adds some delicious protein.

1 large eggplant, diced
2 tablespoons olive
  oil, divided
Kosher salt
Freshly ground black pepper
2 tablespoons tahini
Juice of 1 lemon
1 garlic clove, smashed
1 teaspoon ground cumin
1 teaspoon ground sumac
2 ounces smoked
  salmon, chopped
¼ cup chopped fresh parsley

1. Preheat the oven to 400°F. Line a baking sheet with aluminum foil or parchment paper.

2. In a small bowl, toss the eggplant with 1 tablespoon of oil and salt and black pepper to taste. Transfer to the prepared baking sheet, making sure the eggplant is in a single layer. Bake for 40 minutes.

3. Once the eggplant is finished baking, carefully transfer it to a blender or food processor. Add the remaining 1 tablespoon of olive oil, tahini, lemon juice, garlic, cumin, and sumac. Blend until smooth. Add the salmon and parsley, reserving just a pinch of parsley for garnish. Pulse until both are incorporated.

4. Garnish with the reserved parsley and serve.

Serving suggestion: Serve this with toasted pita chips if you are not concerned about carbs. Or for a healthy swap, use fresh veggies for dipping. I love making a crudité platter with this dip in the middle, surrounded by sugar snap peas, radish slices, cherry tomatoes, carrots, celery, and jicama sticks.

PER SERVING: Calories: 108; Total Fat: 8g; Saturated Fat: 1g; Omega-3 Fat: 155mg; Cholesterol: 2mg; Sodium: 227mg; Total Carbohydrates: 7g; Fiber: 3g; Sugars: 3g; Protein: 4g

Baked Avocado Fries with Chipotle Aioli

SERVES 4 / PREP TIME: 10 MINUTES / COOK TIME: 15 MINUTES

I love avocados and fries separately, so naturally this is one of my favorite recipes because they are combined. They're crispy on the outside and warm and creamy on the inside.

3 ripe avocados
1 cup all-purpose flour
1 teaspoon ground cumin
1 teaspoon paprika
Kosher salt
2 eggs, beaten
1 cup whole-wheat panko
   bread crumbs
¼ cup mayonnaise
½ cup 2% plain Greek yogurt
1 chipotle chile in
   adobo sauce
Juice of ½ lemon
1 teaspoon grated
   lemon zest
½ teaspoon paprika

1. Preheat the oven to 400°F. Line a baking sheet with aluminum foil or parchment paper.

2. Cut the avocados in half and take the pits out. Peel the avocado and cut each half into 4 or 5 slices.

3. In a bowl, mix the flour with the cumin and paprika, and season with salt. Put the eggs in another bowl and the bread crumbs in a third bowl. Dredge 1 slice of avocado in the flour mixture, followed by the eggs, and then the bread crumbs, and place it on the prepared baking sheet. Repeat with the remaining avocado slices. Bake for 15 minutes, flipping halfway through.

4. While the avocado fries are baking, make the aioli by adding the mayonnaise, yogurt, chipotle chile with 1 tablespoon of the adobo sauce, lemon juice, lemon zest, paprika, and salt to taste to a food processor or blender. Blend until smooth. Serve!

Serving suggestion: Pair these avocado fries with Baked Fish Sticks with Easy Honey Mustard (page 106). They have some of the same ingredients, making it easy to prepare the two recipes at the same time.

PER SERVING: Calories: 554; Total Fat: 30g; Saturated Fat: 5g; Omega-3 Fat: 189mg; Cholesterol: 88mg; Sodium: 369mg; Total Carbohydrates: 61g; Fiber: 12g; Sugars: 11g; Protein: 14g

Roasted Carrots with Spiced Yogurt and Granola

SERVES 4 TO 6 / PREP TIME: 10 MINUTES / COOK TIME: 30 MINUTES

Sweet roasted carrots paired with creamy yogurt and crunchy granola . . . need I say more? This may not be a combo you are familiar with, but after trying one bite, you will be hooked!

1 bunch tricolored carrots, trimmed and peeled
1 tablespoon olive oil
2 tablespoons honey, divided
Kosher salt
Freshly ground black pepper
½ cup 2% plain Greek yogurt
2 teaspoons finely chopped fresh rosemary
Juice of 1 lemon
½ cup of your favorite granola

1. Preheat the oven to 400°F. Line a baking sheet with aluminum foil or parchment paper.

2. Place the carrots, olive oil, 1 tablespoon of honey, and salt and black pepper to taste in a rectangular dish. Toss to coat the carrots. Transfer the carrots to the prepared baking sheet and bake for 25 to 30 minutes, until slightly caramelized and golden.

3. In a bowl, combine the yogurt, rosemary, lemon juice, and remaining 1 tablespoon of honey.

4. To serve, place 3 or 4 carrots on each plate. Add a dollop of yogurt and a spoonful of granola. Serve warm.

Serving suggestion: It's time to get crunching! For the perfect bite, make sure to cut the carrots, then dip each forkful in yogurt and coat it in granola. I love pairing this side dish with Pistachio-Crusted Salmon (page 94). You can bake the salmon fillets and the carrots at the same time for a quick and easy dinner.

PER SERVING: Calories: 158; Total Fat: 5g; Saturated Fat: 1g; Omega-3 Fat: 14mg; Cholesterol: 3mg; Sodium: 131mg; Total Carbohydrates: 26g; Fiber: 4g; Sugars: 17g; Protein: 5g

Tuna and Hummus Stuffed Mini Peppers

SERVES 4 / PREP TIME: 10 MINUTES

If you haven't done so already, you need to try mixing tuna with hummus instead of mayonnaise. Hummus offers the perfect creamy consistency but with more flavor than mayonnaise. It also has higher fiber and protein, and depending which brand you choose, it can also have fewer calories. Use your favorite flavor of hummus. I love roasted red pepper, garlic, and olive hummus.

1 (5-ounce) can tuna packed in water, drained

¼ cup hummus

1 celery stalk, finely chopped

¼ red onion, finely chopped

12 tricolored mini bell peppers, seeded, deveined, and halved plus 1 mini bell pepper, seeded, deveined, and finely chopped

1. In a large mixing bowl, mix together the tuna, hummus, celery, and red onion.

2. Place the pepper halves on a serving tray.

3. Using a spoon, stuff the mini pepper halves with the tuna-hummus mixture. Sprinkle with the chopped mini pepper.

Variation tip: You can also drizzle the stuffed peppers with your favorite balsamic glaze, if you desire. If you are in a rush, save time and mix together the tuna and hummus without the additional chopped vegetables. Enjoy this mixture on top of a salad, in a pita pocket, or as a dip for your favorite veggies.

PER SERVING: Calories: 193; Total Fat: 2g; Saturated Fat: 0g; Omega-3 Fat: 99mg; Cholesterol: 37mg; Sodium: 380mg; Total Carbohydrates: 18g; Fiber: 4g; Sugars: 9g; Protein: 24g

Butternut Squash Mac and Cheese

SERVES 6 TO 8 / PREP TIME: 10 MINUTES / COOK TIME: 1 HOUR 15 MINUTES

Mac and cheese is one of my favorite comfort foods. Despite the lack of butter and cream in this dish, it is still just as comforting as the traditional version, but definitely on the lighter side.

3 cups cubed
   butternut squash
1 yellow onion, cut into
   8 pieces
2 tablespoons olive oil
1 teaspoon ground cumin
2 teaspoons ground
   turmeric
½ teaspoon ground
   cayenne pepper
Kosher salt
Freshly ground black pepper
12 ounces elbow pasta
1 cup grated sharp
   cheddar cheese
1 cup grated Gruyère cheese
1 cup 1% milk
½ cup whole-wheat panko
   bread crumbs

1. Preheat the oven to 400°F. Line a rimmed baking sheet with aluminum foil or parchment paper.

2. In a large mixing bowl, put the butternut squash, onion, olive oil, cumin, turmeric, cayenne pepper, and salt and black pepper to taste. Mix until evenly coated, and transfer to the prepared baking sheet. Bake for 40 minutes, until the squash is soft.

3. While the squash is baking, cook the pasta according to the package instructions.

4. Mix the cheddar and Gruyère cheeses together in a bowl.

5. Once the squash is done, remove it from the oven and turn the oven down to 375°F. Let the squash cool for a few minutes and carefully transfer it to a blender. Blend on high until smooth.

6. In a large pot over medium heat, bring the butternut squash purée to a simmer. Add the milk and stir in 1½ cups of the cheese. Taste and adjust the seasoning as needed. Once the cheese is melted, add the cooked pasta. Stir to combine.

7. Pour the pasta mixture into a 9-by-13-inch baking dish and spread evenly. Sprinkle the remaining ½ cup cheese and the bread crumbs on top. Cover the dish with aluminum foil and bake for 30 minutes.

8. After 30 minutes, carefully remove the foil, turn the broiler on, and broil the mac and cheese for 2 to 3 minutes, until the cheese is slightly browned and crispy.

9. Once done cooking, allow the mac and cheese to sit uncovered for 10 minutes before serving.

Variation tip: Easily make this gluten-free by using your favorite gluten-free pasta and bread crumbs. Or make this dish vegan by using an unsweetened nut milk and your favorite dairy-free cheese.

PER SERVING: Calories: 367; Total Fat: 18g; Saturated Fat: 9g; Omega-3 Fat: 194mg; Cholesterol: 43mg; Sodium: 235mg; Total Carbohydrates: 35g; Fiber: 4g; Sugars: 5g; Protein: 16g

Spiced Crab Guacamole

SERVES 6 TO 8 / PREP TIME: 10 MINUTES

This pescatarian-friendly recipe gives your traditional guacamole a little makeover with the addition of spiced crabmeat. This is my signature party appetizer, and it's a crowd favorite. Pair it with your favorite tortilla chips or veggies for dipping.

2 ripe avocados, pitted
   and peeled
1 small red onion,
   finely diced
1 garlic clove, minced
½ cup fresh or frozen
   roasted corn kernels,
   thawed if frozen
½ cup roughly chopped
   fresh cilantro,
   lightly packed
Juice of 1½ limes
Kosher salt
Freshly ground black pepper
½ cup canned lump
   crabmeat, drained
1 tablespoon olive oil
¼ teaspoon ground
   cayenne pepper
¼ teaspoon paprika

1. In a large serving bowl, mash together the avocados, red onion, garlic, corn, cilantro, and lime juice. Season with salt and black pepper.

2. In another bowl, mix together the crabmeat, olive oil, cayenne pepper, paprika, and salt and black pepper to taste.

3. Add the crab mixture to the avocado mixture. Stir to combine. Taste and adjust the seasoning if needed. Serve with tortilla chips or a vegetable crudité platter.

Leftovers: If you have leftovers, squeeze some lemon or lime juice over the guacamole and make sure the dish is covered tightly. This will help keep the avocados from browning.

PER SERVING: Calories: 144; Total Fat: 11g; Saturated Fat: 2g; Omega-3 Fat: 132mg; Cholesterol: 6mg; Sodium: 97mg; Total Carbohydrates: 10g; Fiber: 5g; Sugars: 2g; Protein: 3g

Thai Red Curry Cauliflower "Wings"

SERVES 6 / PREP TIME: 5 MINUTES / COOK TIME: 30 MINUTES

This recipe is another example of the versatility of cauliflower. I made these cauliflower "wings" for a Super Bowl party and let me tell you, they were a hit among all the football fans who usually devour chicken wing after chicken wing—now that says a lot!

1 head cauliflower, cut into large florets

¾ cup coconut cream

2 tablespoons Thai red curry powder or paste

1. Preheat the oven to 400°F. Line a rimmed baking sheet with aluminum foil or parchment paper.

2. Place the cauliflower florets in a large mixing bowl. Set aside.

3. In a medium saucepan over medium to high heat, combine the coconut cream and curry powder. Stir together until simmering, then pour the mixture over the cauliflower florets. Toss until evenly coated.

4. Spread out the cauliflower florets evenly on the prepared baking sheet. Bake for 25 to 30 minutes. Serve warm.

Substitution tip: In place of Thai red curry powder (or paste) and coconut cream, you can use ¾ cup premade Thai red curry sauce.

Always check ingredient packaging for gluten-free labeling.

PER SERVING: Calories: 169; Total Fat: 6g; Saturated Fat: 6g; Omega-3 Fat: 78mg; Cholesterol: 0mg; Sodium: 57mg; Total Carbohydrates: 27g; Fiber: 2g; Sugars: 22g; Protein: 3g

Roasted Brussels Sprouts with Baked Apples

SERVES 4 / PREP TIME: 5 MINUTES / COOK TIME: 40 MINUTES

I did not like Brussels sprouts as a child. They smelled funny and tasted bitter. Once I started experimenting in the kitchen and cooking Brussels sprouts with a variety of flavors, however, they became one of my favorite veggies.

3 cups Brussels
  sprouts, halved
1 apple, cored and diced
⅓ cup unsweetened
  applesauce
2 tablespoons olive oil
1 tablespoon honey
Kosher salt
Freshly ground black pepper

1. Preheat the oven to 400°F. Line a rimmed baking sheet with aluminum foil or parchment paper.

2. In a large mixing bowl, toss together the Brussels sprouts, apple, applesauce, olive oil, and honey. Season with salt and black pepper.

3. Transfer to the prepared baking sheet. Bake for 30 to 40 minutes, until the Brussels sprouts are slightly browned and crispy.

Leftovers: Store these in an airtight container in the refrigerator for up to 5 days. I love adding the leftovers to a salad the next day with a fresh, cut-up apple for extra juiciness and crunch.

Always check ingredient packaging for gluten-free labeling.

PER SERVING: Calories: 142; Total Fat: 7g; Saturated Fat: 1g; Omega-3 Fat: 66mg; Cholesterol: 0mg; Sodium: 56mg; Total Carbohydrates: 20g; Fiber: 4g; Sugars: 14g; Protein: 3g

Desserts

Protein-Packed Chocolate Mousse, page 147

Strawberry Cheesecake Bites

MAKES 24 BITES / PREP TIME: 15 MINUTES, PLUS 3 HOURS TO FREEZE

I love cheesecake, but sometimes it's too rich to have more than just a few bites. I created these bite-size Greek yogurt and Truwhip mini cheesecakes to be lighter than the original, but just as delicious.

2 cups of your favorite
  trail mix
¼ cup maple syrup
1½ cups 2% vanilla or
  strawberry Greek yogurt
1 cup Truwhip
1 cup cream cheese
1 cup whole
  strawberries, trimmed
½ cup thinly sliced
  strawberries

1. Line a 24-cup mini cupcake pan with paper liners. Set aside.

2. For the crust, put the trail mix and maple syrup in a blender or food processor. Pulse until it is the consistency of a sticky granola. Spoon the trail mix mixture into the bottom of each cupcake liner. Press the crust firmly with your fingers to make sure it creates an even surface. Remove any excess trail mix from the blender and wipe the blender clean.

3. To the same blender or food processor, add the Greek yogurt, Truwhip, cream cheese, and whole strawberries. Blend until smooth. Transfer to a large piping bag or large sealable plastic bag with a small corner cut off. Pipe the Greek yogurt mixture into each cupcake liner until the crust is completely covered.

4. Top each cheesecake bite with a slice of strawberry. Put them in the freezer for 3 to 4 hours, or until completely frozen.

5. Once frozen, thaw for about 15 to 20 minutes at room temperature. Consume while slightly cold.

Ingredient tip: Truwhip is a healthier version of the other premade whipped creams. Don't worry, those old favorites are okay if you cannot find Truwhip in your local grocery store. You can also make this recipe into cheesecake bars by using a 9-by-13-inch cake pan or into an actual round cheesecake by using a circular 8-inch cake pan. Make this gluten-free by using gluten-free granola.

PER SERVING (2 BITES): Calories: 265; Total Fat: 17g; Saturated Fat: 9g; Omega-3 Fat: 34mg; Cholesterol: 23mg; Sodium: 129mg; Total Carbohydrates: 24g; Fiber: 0g; Sugars: 10g; Protein: 7g

Roasted Figs with Honey and Mascarpone Cheese

SERVES 4 TO 6 / PREP TIME: 10 MINUTES / COOK TIME: 20 MINUTES

I have so many health-conscious friends and we all want the same thing: sweetness from something real instead of from a sugar-laden dessert that puts you in a food coma. These figs are naturally sweet, and once paired with the creaminess of the mascarpone cheese topping, you will get the fairy-tale ending to your dinner party that you've always dreamed of.

12 dried figs, halved

1 tablespoon olive oil

2 tablespoons honey, divided

1 teaspoon finely chopped fresh rosemary

¼ teaspoon sea salt, plus more for serving

2 cups 2% plain regular or Greek yogurt

¾ cup mascarpone cheese

1 teaspoon ground cinnamon

1 teaspoon vanilla extract

1. Preheat the oven to 375°F. Line a baking sheet with aluminum foil or parchment paper.

2. In a large bowl, combine the figs, olive oil, 1 tablespoon of honey, rosemary, and sea salt. Toss until fully coated. Transfer to the prepared baking sheet, placing each fig cut-side up. Bake for 15 to 20 minutes.

3. While the figs bake, mix together the yogurt, mascarpone cheese, cinnamon, and vanilla. Evenly divide the yogurt mixture among individual bowls. Once the figs are finished baking, place 4 to 6 fig halves into each bowl along with a spoonful of the drippings from the baking sheet. Drizzle with the remaining 1 tablespoon of honey. Top with a pinch of sea salt before serving.

Ingredient tip: Add a little extra sweetness by using vanilla yogurt—this is dessert, so why not?!

PER SERVING: Calories: 315; Total Fat: 16g; Saturated Fat: 1g; Omega-3 Fat: 30mg; Cholesterol: 7mg; Sodium: 116mg; Total Carbohydrates: 35g; Fiber: 4g; Sugars: 26g; Protein: 10g

Chocolate Hummus

SERVES 6 TO 8 / PREP TIME: 10 MINUTES, PLUS 45 MINUTES TO CHILL

Don't be fooled! Although this is called hummus, it's made with chocolate, so it's sweet instead of savory. You must try this—you'll be amazed at how sweet and delicious it tastes.

1 (15-ounce) can no-salt-added chickpeas, rinsed and drained
1 tablespoon coconut oil
⅓ cup Nutella
¼ cup chocolate coconut milk
2 tablespoons cocoa powder
¼ teaspoon sea salt

Put the chickpeas, coconut oil, Nutella, chocolate coconut milk, cocoa powder, and salt in a blender or food processor. Blend until smooth. Transfer to a bowl and refrigerate for 45 to 60 minutes, until chilled. Serve cold.

Serving suggestion: Enjoy this hummus with your favorite fruits, like strawberries or peaches.

Always check ingredient packaging for gluten-free labeling.

PER SERVING: Calories: 268; Total Fat: 14g; Saturated Fat: 6g; Omega-3 Fat: 24mg; Cholesterol: 0mg; Sodium: 101mg; Total Carbohydrates: 30g; Fiber: 5g; Sugars: 19g; Protein: 6g

Brownie Cake Pops

MAKES 12 TO 14 CAKE POPS / PREP TIME: 20 MINUTES,
PLUS 1 HOUR 45 MINUTES TO CHILL / COOK TIME: 25 MINUTES

I used to always make black bean and avocado brownies. Then my daughter's love for cake pops gave me the idea to make these healthy cake pops using my favorite brownie recipe. For this recipe you will need 12 to 14 lollipop sticks, as well as a Styrofoam block or brick at least 12 inches long by 4 inches wide, available from a craft store.

Cooking spray

1 (15-ounce) can
no-salt-added black
beans, drained and rinsed

1 ripe avocado, peeled
and pitted

2 eggs

½ cup brown sugar

½ cup cocoa powder

¼ cup hazelnuts,
finely chopped

1 tablespoon coconut oil

¼ teaspoon sea salt

2 teaspoons vanilla extract

½ teaspoon baking powder

¼ teaspoon baking soda

1 cup chocolate
chips, melted

3 tablespoons coconut
oil, melted

1. Preheat the oven to 350°F. Coat an 8-by-8-inch baking dish with cooking spray.

2. Put the black beans, avocado, eggs, brown sugar, cocoa powder, hazelnuts, coconut oil, sea salt, vanilla, baking powder, and baking soda in a high-powered blender or food processor. Blend until very smooth. Transfer to the prepared baking dish and bake for 20 to 23 minutes, or until the center is fully cooked. Let cool and refrigerate for 45 minutes.

3. Remove the brownie cake from the refrigerator. Crumble into a large mixing bowl and mash up.

4. Line a large baking sheet with parchment paper. Set aside.

5. Using your hands, roll about a tablespoon of the mashed brownie cake into a compact ball the size of a ping-pong ball. Repeat until you have 12 to 14 balls. ➤

6. Prepare the coating by mixing the melted chocolate and melted coconut oil together in a small bowl. Dip one end of a lollipop stick into the melted chocolate. Pierce a cake ball with the chocolate-coated end of the stick. Place it carefully on the prepared baking sheet. Repeat with the rest of the lollipop sticks and cake balls. Transfer to the refrigerator and chill for 30 minutes.

7. Remelt the chocolate in the microwave until smooth. Using a spoon, coat each cake pop with chocolate. Once coated, sprinkle with the chopped hazelnuts. Insert the cake pop sticks into the Styrofoam block, leaving space between each.

8. Refrigerate for 30 minutes, until the chocolate hardens.

Variation tip: Get creative with the toppings. Use your favorite chopped nuts or even coconut flakes.

Always check ingredient packaging for gluten-free labeling.

PER SERVING (2 CAKE POPS): Calories: 279; Total Fat: 19g; Saturated Fat: 11g; Omega-3 Fat: 30mg; Cholesterol: 30mg; Sodium: 93mg; Total Carbohydrates: 28g; Fiber: 5g; Sugars: 18g; Protein: 6g

Baked Pears Stuffed with Yogurt and Granola

SERVES 4 / PREP TIME: 5 MINUTES / COOK TIME: 20 MINUTES

I love eating fruit as dessert, especially when it's baked. Baking fruit really brings out its natural sweetness. This dessert is one of my favorites because it's light, healthy, and super satisfying.

4 ripe pears, halved

1 tablespoon olive oil

1 tablespoon pure
   maple syrup

2 teaspoons ground
   cinnamon

1 cup 2% plain regular or
   Greek yogurt

½ cup of your
   favorite granola

Sea salt

1. Preheat the oven to 375°F. Line a baking sheet with aluminum foil or parchment paper.

2. Using a spoon, scoop out the center of each pear half, making sure to remove the seeds. Transfer the pears cut-side up to the baking sheet. Brush the pears with the olive oil. Add a drizzle of maple syrup and a dash of cinnamon to each half. Bake for 20 minutes.

3. Once done baking, carefully transfer 2 pear halves to each plate. Add a few tablespoons of Greek yogurt to the centers, followed by a hearty spoonful of granola. Sprinkle with a pinch of sea salt before serving.

Substitution tip: Make this gluten-free by using gluten-free granola.

PER SERVING: Calories: 234; Total Fat: 5g; Saturated Fat: 2g; Omega-3 Fat: 42mg; Cholesterol: 5mg; Sodium: 90mg; Total Carbohydrates: 43g; Fiber: 6g; Sugars: 27g; Protein: 7g

Strawberry Mug Cake

SERVES 2 / PREP TIME: 5 MINUTES / COOK TIME: 1 MINUTE 30 SECONDS

When I first tried this mug cake, it was love at first bite. I'm excited to share this recipe because I know it will be love at first bite for you, too!

2 tablespoons 2% plain Greek yogurt
1 tablespoon mascarpone cheese
Pinch ground cinnamon
1½ teaspoons vanilla extract, divided
¼ cup all-purpose flour
2 tablespoons coconut sugar
⅛ teaspoon baking powder
⅛ teaspoon baking soda
3 tablespoons 1% milk
2 teaspoons coconut oil, melted
4 strawberries, trimmed and halved, plus 2 strawberries, trimmed and sliced
Cooking spray

1. To make the topping, in a medium bowl, mix together the Greek yogurt, mascarpone cheese, cinnamon, and ½ teaspoon of vanilla. Set aside.

2. In another medium bowl, whisk together the flour, coconut sugar, baking powder, and baking soda. Make a well in the center and add the remaining 1 teaspoon of vanilla, milk, and coconut oil. Fold in the halved strawberries.

3. Coat a large mug or two small mugs with cooking spray. Pour the batter into the mug, leaving at least 1 inch of room from the top.

4. Microwave for 1 minute 30 seconds, or until the mug cake rises and is cooked through.

5. Once cooked, carefully remove the mug cake from the microwave. Add a few spoonfuls of the topping. Sprinkle with the sliced strawberries and enjoy.

Variation tip: Please note that every microwave will cook this cake differently. Pay close attention as you cook it to make sure you don't under- or overcook it. You can also use buckwheat flour as a gluten-free alternative. Buckwheat flour is denser, so the cake will come out less fluffy and will have a nuttier flavor.

PER SERVING: Calories: 208; Total Fat: 9g; Saturated Fat: 6g; Omega-3 Fat: 17mg; Cholesterol: 12mg; Sodium: 687mg; Total Carbohydrates: 28g; Fiber: 1g; Sugars: 15g; Protein: 4g

Protein-Packed Chocolate Mousse

SERVES 4 / PREP TIME: 10 MINUTES, PLUS 30 MINUTES TO CHILL

I love being sneaky with tofu and hiding it in foods where no one would ever suspect it. It takes on the flavor of all the other ingredients. When I make this mousse, I feel like the ultimate sneaky chef.

½ cup chocolate chips or 4 ounces of your favorite chocolate, chopped

½ (16-ounce) package silken tofu

⅓ cup cocoa powder

2 teaspoons vanilla extract

Berries of your choice, for garnish (optional)

Fresh mint, for garnish (optional)

Shaved chocolate, for garnish (optional)

1. Melt the chocolate chips on the stove using a double boiler, or in the microwave in a microwave-safe bowl.

2. Transfer the melted chocolate to a food processor. Add the tofu, cocoa powder, and vanilla. Blend until smooth.

3. Scoop into 4 dishes. Refrigerate for 30 minutes. To serve, garnish with berries, mint, and shaved chocolate, if you desire.

Ingredient tip: Using silken tofu will you give you more of a pudding consistency. If you want a thicker mousse, use firm or extra-firm tofu.

Always check ingredient packaging for gluten-free labeling.

PER SERVING: Calories: 204; Total Fat: 11g; Saturated Fat: 7g; Omega-3 Fat: 2mg; Cholesterol: 7mg; Sodium: 30mg; Total Carbohydrates: 22g; Fiber: 4g; Sugars: 15g; Protein: 7g

Cookieless Cookie Dough

SERVES 6 TO 8 / PREP TIME: 10 MINUTES, PLUS 1 HOUR TO CHILL

As a kid, I used to love sneaking a few bites of cookie dough whenever anyone was baking cookies. That stopped, of course, once I learned about the dangers of eating raw eggs. So, I created a cookie dough that is meant to be eaten by the spoonful. It's a dream come true!

1 (15-ounce) can no-salt-added chickpeas, rinsed and drained

¼ cup of your favorite nut butter

3 tablespoons brown sugar

1 tablespoon vanilla extract

⅓ cup chocolate chips

1. Place the chickpeas, nut butter, brown sugar, and vanilla in a blender or food processor. Blend until smooth.

2. Transfer to a mixing bowl. Fold in the chocolate chips. Cover and refrigerate for 1 hour.

3. Serve cold and enjoy by the spoonful or as a spread between two graham crackers.

Variation tip: I love using all types of nut butters to make this recipe. Sometimes I use peanut butter, but other times I'll use almond butter or cashew butter.

Always check ingredient packaging for gluten-free labeling.

PER SERVING: Calories: 195; Total Fat: 10g; Saturated Fat: 4g; Omega-3 Fat: 14mg; Cholesterol: 0mg; Sodium: 54mg; Total Carbohydrates: 22g; Fiber: 3g; Sugars: 9g; Protein: 7g

The Dirty Dozen™ and the Clean Fifteen™

A nonprofit environmental watchdog organization called Environmental Working Group (EWG) looks at data supplied by the U.S. Department of Agriculture (USDA) and the Food and Drug Administration (FDA) about pesticide residues. Each year it compiles a list of the best and worst pesticide loads found in commercial crops. You can use these lists to decide which fruits and vegetables to buy organic to minimize your exposure to pesticides and which produce is considered safe enough to buy conventionally. This does not mean they are pesticide-free, though, so wash these fruits and vegetables thoroughly.

Dirty Dozen™	Clean Fifteen™
apples	asparagus
celery	avocados
cherries	broccoli
grapes	cabbages
nectarines	cantaloupes
peaches	cauliflower
pears	eggplants
potatoes	honeydew melons
spinach	kiwis
strawberries	mangoes
sweet bell peppers	onions
tomatoes	papayas
	pineapples
*Additionally, nearly three-quarters of hot pepper samples contained pesticide residues	sweet corn
	sweet peas (frozen)

Measurement Conversions

Oven Temperatures

Fahrenheit (F)	Celsius (C) (approx.)
250°F	120°C
300°F	150°C
325°F	165°C
350°F	180°C
375°F	190°C
400°F	200°C
425°F	220°C
450°F	230°C

Volume Equivalents (Liquid)

Standard	US Standard (oz.)	Metric (approx.)
2 tablespoons	1 fl. oz.	30 mL
¼ cup	2 fl. oz.	60 mL
½ cup	4 fl. oz.	120 mL
1 cup	8 fl. oz.	240 mL
1½ cups	12 fl. oz.	355 mL
2 cups or 1 pint	16 fl. oz.	475 mL
4 cups or 1 quart	32 fl. oz.	1 L
1 gallon	128 fl. oz.	4 L

Weight Equivalents

Standard	Metric (approx.)
½ ounce	15 g
1 ounce	30 g
2 ounces	60 g
4 ounces	115 g
8 ounces	225 g
12 ounces	340 g
16 ounces or 1 pound	455 g

Volume Equivalents (Dry)

Standard	Metric (approx.)
⅛ teaspoon	0.5 mL
¼ teaspoon	1 mL
½ teaspoon	2 mL
¾ teaspoon	4 mL
1 teaspoon	5 mL
1 tablespoon	15 mL
¼ cup	59 mL
⅓ cup	79 mL
½ cup	118 mL
⅔ cup	156 mL
¾ cup	177 mL
1 cup	235 mL
2 cups or 1 pint	475 mL
3 cups	700 mL
4 cups or 1 quart	1 L

Resources

Monterey Bay Aquarium Seafood Watch

There is a lot to consider and remember when it comes to purchasing sustainable seafood. The nonprofit Monterey Bay Aquarium Seafood Watch will steer you in the right direction and help you buy seafood that is caught and raised using practices that have less impact on the environment. They offer a free, super helpful app called the Seafood Watch App, which categorizes different seafood as "best choice" or "good alternative" and tells you what kinds should be avoided.

Website: http://www.seafoodwatch.org

The Marine Conservation Society

This organization has a wonderful seasonal fish-buying guide that I use to make sure that I save money and get a better-quality product when I buy seafood in my local store.

Link: https://www.mcsuk.org/media/seafood/BuyingFishInSeason.pdf

EDF Seafood Selector

This website from the Environmental Defense Fund is another online seafood guide that categorizes the best choices, okay choices, and worst choices when it comes to eating fish sustainably.

Website: http://seafood.edf.org

The Environmental Protection Agency (EPA)

The EPA is an agency that develops and enforces regulations to help protect human and environmental health. This agency, along with the Food and Drug Administration, issues advice on eating fish, especially for pregnant or breastfeeding women, women who may become pregnant, and children. It developed an easy-to-read, consumer-friendly infographic titled "Eating Fish: What Pregnant Women and Parents Should Know."

Infographic: https://www.epa.gov/fish-tech/2017-epa-fda-advice-about-eating-fish-and-shellfish

Food and Drug Administration

This government agency regulates and overseas food, drugs, medical devices, and cosmetic products. It offers up-to-date safety information on how to properly buy, prepare, store, and cook fish and shellfish.

Link: https://www.fda.gov/food/resourcesforyou/consumers/ucm077331.htm

Ocean Conservancy

This agency finds science-based solutions to conserve the health and vitality of the ocean and its habitat. It supports sustainable fisheries and offers consumer-friendly information through its wildlife fact sheets.

Website: https://oceanconservancy.org

EcoWatch

EcoWatch is a leading environmental news site that publishes articles to communicate and engage with millions of consumers who share the same interest of ensuring the longevity and health of our planet. Sign up for their e-mail newsletters to stay up-to-date on hot topics that affect both our health and the environment.

Website: https://www.ecowatch.com

Harvard T. H. Chan School of Public Health

The Harvard School of Public Health offers consumer-friendly information on various health topics, such as recommendations for omega-3 intake. If you like reading about hot topics in health, I would recommend signing up for its e-mail newsletter.

Website: https://www.hsph.harvard.edu/nutritionsource

Agency for Toxic Substances and Disease Registry

This agency offers an in-depth overview of the various concerns over mercury.

Website: https://www.atsdr.cdc.gov/toxfaqs/tf.asp?id=113&tid=24

Seafood Health Facts

This is a great resource to help you balance the benefits and risks of seafood consumption. This website was developed by Cornell University and the New York Sea Grant Extension program and also collaborates with a number of other universities.

Website: https://www.seafoodhealthfacts.org/seafood-safety/general-information -patients-and-consumers

The Kitchn

This is my go-to website for learning new cooking techniques. For visual learners, like myself, it offers videos on how to prepare and cook various items.

Website: https://www.thekitchn.com

These two brands are known for sustainable fishing practices and transparency.

Wild Planet

http://www.wildplanetfoods.com

Wild Selections

http://wildselections.com

References

Barnard, N. D., S. M. Levin, and Y. Yokoyama. 2015. "A Systematic Review and Meta-analysis of Changes in Body Weight in Clinical Trials of Vegetarian Diets." *Journal of the Academy of Nutrition and Dietetics* 115 (6): 954–69.

Burr, M. L., A. M. Fehily, J. F. Gilbert, S. Rogers, R. M. Holliday, P. M. Sweetnam, et al. 1989. "Effects of Changes in Fat, Fish, and Fibre Intakes on Death and Myocardial Reinfarction: Diet and Reinfarction Trial (DART)." *Lancet* 2 (8666): 757–61.

Del Gobbo, L. C., F. Imamura, S. Aslibekyan, M. Marklund, J. K. Virtanen, M. Wennberg, et al. 2016. "Omega-3 Polyunsaturated Fatty Acid Biomarkers and Coronary Heart Disease: Pooling Project of 19 Cohort Studies." *JAMA Internal Medicine* 176:1155–66.

Djousse, L., A. O. Akinkuolie, J. H. Wu, E. L. Ding, and J. M. Gaziano. 2012. "Fish Consumption, Omega-3 Fatty Acids and Risk of Heart Failure: A Meta-analysis." *Clinical Nutrition* 31:846–53.

Harvard Women's Health Watch. "Foods That Fight Inflammation." Last modified August 13, 2017. https://www.health.harvard.edu/staying-healthy /foods-that-fight-inflammation.

Huang, R. Y., C. C. Huang, F. B. Hu, and J. E. Chavarro. 2016. "Vegetarian Diets and Weight Reduction: A Meta-analysis of Randomized Controlled Trials." *Journal of General Internal Medicine* 31 (1): 109–16.

Sekikawa, Akira, J. David Curb, Hirotsugu Ueshima, Aiman El-Saed, Takashi Kadowaki, Robert D. Abbott, et al. 2008. "Marine-Derived n-3 Fatty Acids and Atherosclerosis in Japanese, Japanese Americans, and Whites: A Cross-Sectional Study." *Journal of the American College of Cardiology* 52 (6): 417–24. doi:10.1016/j.jacc.2008.03.047.

Spencer, E. A., P. N. Appleby, G. K. Davey, and T. J. Key. 2003. "Diet and Body Mass Index in 38000 EPIC-Oxford Meat-Eaters, Fish-Eaters, Vegetarians and Vegans." *International Journal of Obesity and Related Metabolic Disorders* 27 (6): 728–34.

Sydenham, E., A. D. Dangour, and W. S. Lim. 2012. "Omega 3 Fatty Acid for the Prevention of Cognitive Decline and Dementia." *Cochrane Database of Systematic Reviews* 6:CD005379. doi:10.1002/14651858.CD005379.pub3.

Tonstad, S., K. Stewart, K. Oda, M. Batech, R. P. Herring, and G. E. Fraser. 2013. "Vegetarian Diets and Incidence of Diabetes in the Adventist Health Study-2." *Nutrition, Metabolism and Cardiovascular Diseases* 23 (4): 292–99.

U.S. Department of Agriculture. "USDA Food Composition Databases." Accessed October 14, 2018. https://ndb.nal.usda.gov/ndb/nutrients/index.

U.S. Department of Health and Human Services and U.S. Department of Agriculture. 2015. 2015–2020 *Dietary Guidelines for Americans.* 8th ed. Washington, DC: Author. https://health.gov/dietaryguidelines/2015/guidelines/.

van Gelder, B. M., M. Tijhuis, S. Kalmijn, and D. Kromhout. 2007. "Fish Consumption, n-3 Fatty Acids, and Subsequent 5-y Cognitive Decline in Elderly Men: The Zutphen Elderly Study." *American Journal of Clinical Nutrition* 85:1142–47.

Recipe Index

Index

About the Author

Nicole Hallissey, MS, RDN, CDN, is a nationally recognized registered dietitian nutritionist, writer, speaker, and owner of Worksite Wellness Nutrition. Primarily based in New York City, Nicole specializes in corporate wellness and has a social media presence as the Worksite Wellness Nutritionist on Instagram. Nicole completed her master's degree in nutrition and education at Columbia University and holds an undergraduate degree in nutrition and dietetics from Rutgers University. She loves creating easy and healthy recipes that align with the schedules of busy, working individuals. Nicole values and preaches the importance of self-care and work–life balance. During her free time, she enjoys traveling, exploring the New York City food scene, and snuggling up for movie nights with her daughter, Leila.

CPSIA information can be obtained
at www.ICGtesting.com
Printed in the USA
LVHW072118131218
600372LV00001B/1/P

9 781641 523127